Successful Global Collaborations in Higher Education Institutions

Abdulrahman Al-Youbi • Adnan H. M. Zahed •
William G. Tierney
Editors

Successful Global Collaborations in Higher Education Institutions

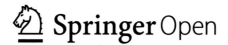

Editors
Abdulrahman Al-Youbi
King Abdulaziz University (KAU)
Jeddah, Saudi Arabia

Adnan H. M. Zahed
King Abdulaziz University
Jeddah, Saudi Arabia

William G. Tierney
Pullias Center for Higher Education
University of Southern California
Los Angeles, USA

ISBN 978-3-030-25524-4   ISBN 978-3-030-25525-1 (eBook)
https://doi.org/10.1007/978-3-030-25525-1

© The Editor(s) (if applicable) and The Author(s) 2020. This book is an open access publication.
Open Access This book is licensed under the terms of the Creative Commons Attribution 4.0 International License (http://creativecommons.org/licenses/by/4.0/), which permits use, sharing, adaptation, distribution and reproduction in any medium or format, as long as you give appropriate credit to the original author(s) and the source, provide a link to the Creative Commons license and indicate if changes were made.
The images or other third party material in this book are included in the book's Creative Commons license, unless indicated otherwise in a credit line to the material. If material is not included in the book's Creative Commons license and your intended use is not permitted by statutory regulation or exceeds the permitted use, you will need to obtain permission directly from the copyright holder.
The use of general descriptive names, registered names, trademarks, service marks, etc. in this publication does not imply, even in the absence of a specific statement, that such names are exempt from the relevant protective laws and regulations and therefore free for general use.
The publisher, the authors and the editors are safe to assume that the advice and information in this book are believed to be true and accurate at the date of publication. Neither the publisher nor the authors or the editors give a warranty, expressed or implied, with respect to the material contained herein or for any errors or omissions that may have been made. The publisher remains neutral with regard to jurisdictional claims in published maps and institutional affiliations.

This Springer imprint is published by the registered company Springer Nature Switzerland AG
The registered company address is: Gewerbestrasse 11, 6330 Cham, Switzerland

Acknowledgements

The editors would like to express their sincere appreciation and gratitude to all the contributors. It is also a pleasure to acknowledge the outstanding help of Profs. Mahmoud Nadim Nahas and Ahmad Abousree Hegazy during the course of preparing the manuscripts of the book. Many thanks are also due to Dr. Abdullah Al-Bargi and Mr. Michael Taylor for editing and proofreading the chapters of the book.

Introduction

Universities used to be discrete organizations. Perhaps no more than a dozen universities had global aspirations prior to the twenty-first century. Many universities may have had important implications for the country where they existed, but their roles, governance structures, and organizational structures were relatively clear. Universities taught students from the country where they were situated. Faculty did discrete research that largely focused on national problems (and was funded through national funding). Institutions either were public and supported by the state or they were private and charged student's tuition. The president (or vice chancellor) had a thin staff of administrative assistants who supported the faculty in teaching and conducting research.

Although the modern research university derives from Europe and the USA, universities have existed throughout the world for centuries. Nalanda University in India was a Buddhist center for learning as far back as 427 AD [1]. The University of Ez-Zitouna was established in 737 AD in Qirwan, Tunisia [2]. The Cordoba Mosque was built in Muslim Iberia (Muslim Spain) in 786 AD and later became the greatest university in Europe during the medieval era [3], where Pope Sylvester II studied when he was a bishop [4]. The University of al-Qarawiyyin opened in 859 AD in Fez, Morocco [5], and Al-Azhar University began in Cairo, Egypt, in 970 AD [6]. The University of Bologna came onto the scene in 1088 [7]. Although these early universities had foreign students and faculty, the norm has been that a university serves the needs of the country where it is located. Most of the students and a majority of the faculty were locals.

When a university thought about foreign affairs, the assumption was that they needed to create a "semester abroad" for undergraduate students. By the 1960s, numerous universities had established simple relationships with universities in foreign countries so that students might gain cross-cultural experience. The "semester abroad" was a good advertisement for a university, but the experience was generally for fewer than 10% of the student population, and the costs were negligible.

Faculty also, on occasion, had a sabbatical in a foreign country. The Fulbright Fellowship Program, founded by the US Senator J. William Fulbright in 1946 [8], enabled US faculty to study abroad for a semester or two, and foreign faculty received scholarships to study in the USA. Post-World War II funding programs aimed to provide opportunities for foreign students to study in the USA. However, even these programs were relatively small and circumscribed.

There is no exact point when universities became more invested in international strategies, but the 1980s was a time of significant growth. China recognized that they needed to enhance their system of higher education and began sending thousands of students to the USA and Australia. Many developing countries, including Saudi Arabia, Malaysia, Pakistan, and India sent hundreds of thousands of students to the UK and the USA for quality education, especially for Master's and Doctorate degrees, to prepare them to be faculty in the universities they graduated from. The host countries benefitted from the foreign students who added to the diversity of their institutions and also provided a new revenue stream for them.

By the twenty-first century, two factors became evident. First, higher education was a growth industry. Massification became the norm as numerous countries tried to expand and open tertiary institutions. The knowledge economy demanded an educated citizenry, so new universities developed and more students entered higher education. Many countries had global aspirations to be considered among the top tier of world-class institutions. Second, foreign students generated revenue. Students from abroad generally could afford to pay full tuition; therefore, what was once an informal activity took on more importance. Although foreign student enrollment generated revenue in countries such as the USA and Australia, even small countries, such as Taiwan and Malaysia, recognized that reaching beyond their borders was a good idea. Malaysia wanted to be a hub for Islamic higher education. Taiwan and Hong Kong wanted to be a place for students who wanted to experience China without having to live in China.

The need for this book, however, goes beyond the simple assumption that, to be an international institution, a university simply ships a few students abroad for a semester, or that an influx of students is little more than a new revenue stream. International higher education today is a much more complex undertaking—one that is necessary but not well understood. Universities are no longer discrete entities that have defined geographic borders. Social media and the Internet have enabled a professor in Jeddah (Saudi Arabia), for instance, to co-author a paper in real time with a colleague in, say, New York (USA). A class may be located in Jeddah, but the students may be dispersed throughout the globe. The reality of the twenty-first century is that if a university wishes to gain preeminence within its country, then it needs to look outwardly to the world. A successful citizen of a country is a global citizen who has cultural strength from his/her own country and at the same time is a multicultural citizen of the world. The educated individual is able to interact with individuals from multiple countries on multiple levels.

The purpose of this book is to lend depth to the manifold topics pertaining to global collaboration. We move away from a one-sided assumption that successful collaboration is either "this or that" and instead highlight the various challenges that confront a university's leadership team.

Chapter 1, which is entitled "King Abdulaziz University's Approach to International Collaboration," delineates the strategies King Abdulaziz University (KAU) has employed that helps explain their rise in global rankings. It also highlights the reasons KAU has chosen to collaborate with other academic and research institutes.

Chapters 2, "Creating an Organizational Climate for Global Partnerships," and 3, "Global Citizens for the Twenty-First Century," point out the challenges that exist, how to overcome them, and what role these partnerships play in the mission of a university. The environment in which universities currently exist as framed by globalization is considered, and subsequently how an innovative culture might be established and maintained to enable global partnerships to be implemented and to succeed is discussed in Chap. 2. Chapter 3 then explores the role international partnerships play for universities and how they educate, research, and impact a disruptive future. How international work-integrated learning opportunities are developed will make a difference in the ability of universities to develop talented global leadership.

Chapter 4, "International Cooperation in East Asian Higher Education," concludes Part I by looking at successful cooperation within a region, namely that of Asia. It discusses the rise of Asia, where eastern Asia has become the most attractive region for international cooperation in higher education. Along with its neighboring countries, the region has some of the most talented human resources in the world because Asia has excellent global telecommunications and a free international flow of funds. There is also a substantial transnational flow of commerce, communications, and ideas. In fact, most economies of eastern Asia are market-oriented.

Part II's three chapters consider knowledge transfer, broadly stated. Chapter 5, "International Collaboration as a Catalyst for Change" is a case study of Nanyang Technological University in Singapore, a university that brought about change through successful engagement in international collaboration.

Chapter 6, "Making Ideas Work for Society" provides an intense focus on why cooperation is a necessary ingredient for knowledge transfer and explains how to do it. Ideas arise everywhere, but they are more likely to be the result of organized research as happens in universities or other research institutes. The ideas and the new knowledge, however, may easily remain in the confines of the university halls and rooms. Making them work for society is the topic of Chap. 6, with an emphasis on how university cooperation can contribute in this respect.

The final chapter in Part II, Chap. 7 "Student Exchange: The First Step Toward International Collaboration" offers a twenty-first-century perspective on student exchanges. These often represent the first step toward international collaboration, as the graduates of universities need to have the ability to interact with people from other cultures and different backgrounds in order to be successful in the international labor market and to work effectively in multicultural teams.

Part III includes two chapters that consider how to sustain partnerships. One of the challenges of global partnerships is not just setting them up, but also sustaining them.

Chapter 8, "The Tricky Terrain of Global University Partnerships," offers evidence of the challenges that exist and how to address them. It presents a taxonomy that explains the basic types of collaborations and partnerships that exist and describes their elements, what they have in common, and the ways in which they are distinct. It then discusses the ways in which institutions that have entered into global collaborations and partnerships have both benefitted, and been challenged, by these arrangements.

Chapter 9, "Long-Term Sustainability in Global Higher Education Partnerships," takes a long view with regard to partnerships and asks what kinds of structures need to be put in place to sustain innovation and experiments. It identifies four specific threats to long-term sustainability. These are divergent motivations and goals for the partnership, inadequate planning and funding volatility, leadership turnover and a lack of formal and informal leaders from within the partnership, and poor staff morale as the result of an over-reliance on part-time employment. The chapter then proposes the conditions that can improve the prospects of long-term sustainability for colleges and universities interested in stable, mutually beneficial global partnerships. Finally, the chapter considers the ethical issues pertinent to contemporary global partnerships.

We surely have not covered every aspect of global collaborations and partnerships in our book. What we have done is set the stage for further investigations. The world may not be flat, as Thomas Friedman has suggested, but we are certain that it is smaller. Our interrelatedness behooves us to help universities think through the hurdles we face with regard to global collaboration and then to put in place the ingredients that lead to long-term success.

Abdulrahman AI-Youbi
Adnan H. M. Zahed
William G. Tierney

References

1. Scharfe, H. (2002). *Education in Ancient India (Handbook of Oriental Studies)*. Brill.
2. Deeb M. J., & Al-Zaytuna. (1995). In J. L. Esposito (Ed.), *The oxford encyclopaedia of the modern Islamic world* (Vol. 4). Oxford: Oxford University Press.
3. Khoury, N. N. N. (1996). The meaning of the great Mosque of Cordoba in the Tenth Century. *Muqarnas, 13*, 80–98.
4. Brown, N. M. (2010). *The abacus and the cross: The story of the pope who brought the light of science to the dark ages*. Basic Books.
5. Lulat, Y. G.-M. (2005). *A history of African higher education from antiquity to the present: A critical synthesis studies in higher education*. Greenwood Publishing Group.

6. Jomier, J., & Al- Azhar (Al-Ḏjāmi Al-Azhar). (2010). In P. Bearman, Th. Bianquis, C. E. Bosworth, E. van Donzel, & W. P. Heinrichs (Eds.), *Encyclopaedia of Islam,* (2nd ed.). Brill.
7. Sanz, N., & Bergan, S. (2006). *The heritage of European universities* (2nd ed.), Higher Education Series No. 7, Council of Europe.
8. Johnson, W., & Colligan, F. J. (1965). *The fulbright program: A history.* The University of Chicago Press.

Contents

Part I Implementation of Global Partnerships

1 **King Abdulaziz University's Approach to International Collaboration** 3
Abdulrahman AI-Youbi and Adnan H. M. Zahed

2 **Creating an Organizational Climate for Global Partnerships: Challenges
and Opportunities** 13
William G. Tierney

3 **Global Citizens for the Twenty-First Century: The Role of International
Partnerships in University Education** 23
Fcridun Hamdullahpur

4 **International Cooperation in East Asian Higher Education** 31
Gerard A. Postiglione

Part II International Collaboration and Knowledge Transfer

5 **International Collaboration as a Catalyst for Change: The Case of Nanyang
Technological University, Singapore 2003–2017** 43
Guaning Su

6 **Making Ideas Work for Society: University Cooperation in Knowledge
Transfer** 51
Jozef Ritzen

7 **Student Exchange: The First Step Toward International Collaboration** 63
Abdullah Atalar

Part III Challenges and Sustainability of Global Partnerships

8 **The Tricky Terrain of Global University Partnerships** 75
James Soto Antony and Tara Nicola

9 **Long-Term Sustainability in Global Higher Education Partnerships** 87
Michael Lanford

Editors and Contributors

About the Editors

Prof. Abdulrahman AI-Youbi has been the President of King Abdulaziz University (KAU) since 2016 and a Professor of Chemistry at KAU since 2000. He earned a Ph.D. in Physical Chemistry from Essex University, UK, in 1986. He has also been the President of the International Advisory Board (IAB) of KAU since 2015. Throughout his career, Prof. AI-Youbi has been an active researcher in his specialization, a passionate teacher and an academic administrator. He has participated in many research projects and has published more than 150 papers in ranked scientific journals. He has also supervised many graduate students. He has held a variety of Academic Administrative positions at KAU including Chairman of the Chemistry Department, Vice Dean of the Faculty of Science (1992–1999), Dean of the Faculty of Science (1999–2002), Vice President (2002–2009), and Vice President for Academic Affairs (2009–2016). In 2015–2016, he was Acting President of both KAU and Jeddah University. As President of KAU, Prof. AI-Youbi has devoted his position to strengthening excellence in academics and research with a dedication to developing an innovative culture. Through President AI-Youbi's leadership, KAU has remained the top university, not only in the Kingdom of Saudi Arabia, but also in the Arab World. His current focus is on expanding KAU's lead by continuing to build on its long-standing strengths in education, research, entrepreneurship and community service to the people of the Kingdom of Saudi Arabia.

President AI-Youbi has participated in more than eighty committees, boards, teams, and working groups at the university level as well as at the Ministry of Education level. In particular, he has participated in the committees that have established new universities in the Kingdom, namely Taiba University, Jazan University, Tabuk University, and the Northern Border University. He has also attended many scientific conferences in the Kingdom and abroad.

Prof. Adnan H. M. Zahed has worked as Consultant to the President of King Abdulaziz University (KAU) since 2016 and the Secretary-General of the International Advisory Board (IAB) of KAU since 2010. He was the KAU Vice President for Graduate Studies and Scientific Research (2009–2016), and worked before that as Dean of Graduate Studies (2007–2009), and before that he was Vice Dean in the Faculty of Engineering (1997–2007). Adnan H. M. Zahed has been a full professor in the Chemical Engineering Department at KAU since 1996. He has also worked in industry as General Supervisor (Consultant) in Saudi Badrah Company (Jeddah, KSA, 1995–1996), Deputy General Manager at Savola Food Company in Jeddah (1993–1995), and Deputy CEO of Tasali Company (Jeddah). He holds a B.Sc. in Chemical Engineering from King Fahd University of Petroleum and Minerals, KSA (1976), and a M.S. and Ph.D. in Chemical Engineering from the University of California (Davis), USA (1982). He has published six books and more than 60 papers in international conferences and refereed journals, in addition to more than 75 technical reports written for the bodies who funded his projects. He has also been a co-author of several University Guides such as the Graduate Studies Guide, Applicable Theses Guide, Thesis Writing Guide, Graduate Studies Procedure Guide, Faculty of

Engineering Prospectus, and Annual Report of Research Activities in the Faculty of Engineering. Adnan H. M. Zahed was included in Marquis Who's Who in the World 2006. He has participated in more than 80 committees at departmental, faculty, and university levels at KAU. In addition, he has participated in four academic accreditation meetings in the USA, and in more than 25 local and international conferences, symposia, and forums. Adnan H. M. Zahed has visited a number of American universities as a delegate of the Saudi Ministry of Education.

Prof. William G. Tierney is co-director of the Pullias Center for Higher Education, University Professor and Wilbur-Kieffer Professor of Higher Education at the University of Southern California (USC). He founded and has directed the Pullias Center for 24 years overseeing faculty, staff, postdoctoral scholars, and graduate students. He also has served as Associate Dean for Research and Faculty Affairs at the Rossier College of Education at USC. Among other duties, he has served as an academic dean at a Native American community college, a Peace Corps volunteer in Morocco, a Fulbright Scholar in Central America and Australia, and a Scholar-in-Residence in Malaysia. He recently completed a year's sabbatical as a Fulbright Scholar in India. His recent books include: *Rethinking Education and Poverty*, *The Impact of Culture on Organizational Decision-making, Trust and the Public Good: Examining the Cultural Conditions of Academic Work*, and *Understanding the Rise of For-profit Colleges and Universities*. He has received the Distinguished Research Award from the Association for the Study of Higher Education (ASHE) and from Division J of the American Educational Research Association (AERA). He is a former president of ASHE, is a Fellow and former president of AERA, and is an elected member of the National Academy of Education, a disciplinary society of 200 individuals recognized for their outstanding scholarship and contributions to education. He earned a Master's degree from Harvard University and a Ph.D. from Stanford University. Professor Tierney is a member of the KAU IAB.

About the Contributors

Prof. James Soto Antony serves on the faculty of the Graduate School of Education at Harvard University. He also serves as Faculty Director of Harvard's Higher Education Program, one of the world's leading graduate programs preparing students to become leaders in colleges and universities. Additionally, he serves as Co-Director of the Management Development Program, a flagship program within the Harvard Institutes for Higher Education portfolio that provides higher education leaders with the tools and insight to think more strategically, balance competing demands, and engage in more forward-thinking leadership.

Professor Antony's research and teaching focus on the preparation of forward-thinking leaders in college and university settings. He has published extensively on issues of higher education leadership and management. He lectures and serves as a leadership development advisor at colleges and universities throughout the USA and abroad.

From 1995 to 2012, he held faculty and leadership roles at the University of Washington, including: Professor in Educational Leadership and Policy and Adjunct Professor in Sociology; Associate Vice-Provost and Associate Dean for Academic Affairs in The Graduate School; and Associate Dean for Academic Programs in the College of Education. While at Washington he also was Director for two graduate degree programs (the Graduate Program in Higher Education, and the Intercollegiate Athletic Leadership Program) and founding Executive Director of the Center for Leadership in Athletics.

From 2012 to 2015, he was an Associate Provost for Yale University, where he worked on issues ranging from faculty development and diversity to undergraduate leadership development within Yale College. During this time, he also held a courtesy faculty appointment as Professor Adjunct in the Yale School of Management and served one year as a Visiting Adjunct Professor at Teachers College, Columbia University.

A past Fellow of the American Council on Education and a current Fellow of the Institute of Higher Education at the University of Georgia, he sits on numerous national and international advisory and editorial boards and is a reviewer for several scholarly journals and associations. He earned his baccalaureate degree in Psychology and his master's degree and Ph.D. in Higher Education and Organizational Change, all from UCLA.

Prof. Abdullah Atalar received his B.S. degree from Middle East Technical University, Ankara, Turkey, in 1974 and his M.S. and Ph.D. degrees from Stanford University, Stanford, CA, in 1976 and 1978, respectively, all in Electrical Engineering. From 1978 to 1980, he was first a Postdoctoral Fellow and later an Engineering Research Associate at Stanford University. For about one year, he worked in Hewlett Packard Labs, Palo Alto. From 1980 to 1986, he was on the faculty of the Middle East Technical University as an Assistant Professor. In 1983, on leave from the University, he worked for Ernst Leitz Wetzlar (now Leica) in Wetzlar, Germany. In 1986, he joined the Bilkent University as the chairman of the Electrical and Electronics Engineering Department and served in the founding of the Department where he is currently a Professor. In 1995, he was a Visiting Professor at Stanford University. From 1996 to 2010, he was the Provost of Bilkent University. He is presently the Rector of the same university. Between 2004 and 2011, he served as a member of the Science Board of TUBI-TAK. His current research interests include microwave electronics and micromachined sensors. He was awarded the Science Award of the Turkish Scientific Research Council (TUBITAK) in 1994. He has been a member of the Turkish Academy of Sciences since 1997 and a Fellow of IEEE since 2007. Professor Atalar is a member of the KAU IAB.

Prof. Dr. Feridun Hamdullahpur has served as the President and Vice-Chancellor of the University of Waterloo since 2010. Dr. Hamdullahpur earned an M.Sc. (1979) in Mechanical Engineering from the Technical University of Istanbul and a Ph.D. (1985) in Chemical Engineering from the Technical University of Nova Scotia (TUNS). He was appointed Assistant Professor (1985) at TUNS at the Center for Energy Studies, Associate Professor in TUNS's Department of Mechanical Engineering (1990) and later full Professor of Mechanical Engineering (1995). Dr. Hamdullahpur is currently a Professor in the Department of Mechanical and Mechatronics Engineering at the University of Waterloo, while he serves concurrently as President

Throughout his career, Dr. Hamdullahpur has been an active researcher in thermo-fluids and energy engineering, a passionate teacher and an academic administrator. He has authored hundreds of scientific and academic publications and supervised over 50 graduate students. He was named a Fellow of the Canadian Academy of Engineering in 2014.

As President of the University of Waterloo, Dr. Hamdullahpur has devoted his tenure to fostering excellence in academics and research, with a dedication to developing an innovative culture committed to experiential education. Through President Hamdullahpur's stewardship, the University of Waterloo has remained Canada's most innovative university for 26 consecutive years.

His current focus at the University of Waterloo is expanding its lead in innovation, building on Waterloo's long-standing and emerging strengths in co-operative education, research, entrepreneurship, and equity.

In 2015, President Hamdullahpur was appointed the Chair of the new Leadership Council for Digital Infrastructure, an ambitious initiative to build a world-leading digital infrastructure ecosystem for Canada.

The President continues to serve in many roles on committees and boards. He has been Chair of the Waterloo Global Science Initiative since 2016, an active member of the Sorbonne Université Strategic Orientation Committee since 2014 and a member of the King Abdulaziz University International Advisory Board since 2017.

In acknowledgment of President Hamdullahpur's leadership in education and innovation, he was awarded the Queen Elizabeth II Diamond Jubilee Medal in January 2013. President Hamdullahpur is a member of the KAU IAB.

Michael Lanford is an Assistant Professor of Higher Education at the University of North Georgia. He employs qualitative research methods and a multidisciplinary theoretical perspective to study institutional innovation, globalization, educational equity, and the impact of educational policy on student development. Over the past three years, his research has appeared in the *American Educational Research Journal, Higher Education, Higher Education: Handbook of Theory and Research*, and *Policy Reviews in Higher Education*, among other publications. Currently, he has articles in press with *Educational Forum,* the *Journal of Research on Technology in Education*, and *Qualitative Inquiry.* Additionally, Michael has forthcoming entries on institutional culture for the *Encyclopedia of International Higher Education Systems and Institutions* and life history for the *Sage Encyclopedia of Social Research Methods.* He has received funding to present his research in Canada, Hong Kong, Mexico, Taiwan, the UK, and the USA.

Tara Nicola is a doctoral student at the Harvard Graduate School of Education. Her research focuses on issues concerning access, choice, and equity in higher education. She is especially interested in evaluating policies related to the college admission process.

Prior to studying at Harvard, Tara was a Research Associate at the National Association for College Admission Counseling (NACAC). She worked in various capacities on projects ranging from the impact of school counselors on students' college-going behaviors and the prevalence of state-mandated individualized learning plans to best practices in supporting the transition of international students to postsecondary education. Her work has been featured in Education Week, Inside Higher Ed, and The Chronicle of Higher Education.

Tara holds an M.Sc. in Higher Education with Distinction from the University of Oxford and an B.A. in English from Johns Hopkins University.

Prof. Gerard A. Postiglione is Honorary Professor and Coordinator of the Consortium for Research on Higher Education. He is a Fellow of the American Educational Research Association for his contribution to research. He has published 16 books and over 150 articles and chapters. He is the editor of the journal *Chinese Education and Society* and a four-book series about education in China. He received the Humanities and Social Science Prestigious Fellow Award from the Hong Kong Research Grants Council and a Lifetime Contribution Award from the Comparative and International Education Society for studies in higher education. His autobiography was published in Leaders in the Sociology of Education (2017), followed by a special collection of his work in 2018. He has done policy research for the Asian Development Bank, the Organization of Economic Cooperation and Development, the United Nations Development Programme, the World Bank, and other international agencies. He was a senior consultant for the Ford Foundation for one year and advised the Carnegie Foundation for the Advancement of Teaching in the academic profession. His contribution to policy reports was received by China's National Reform and Development Commission, State Education Commission and Ministry of Education. He directed the Wah Ching Centre of Research on Education in China for 10 years. In the media, he has appeared on CNN and China's CCTV, has written for The New York Times and The Washington Post, and has been quoted in The New York Times, Wall Street Journal, and other publications such as Science,

Bloomberg BusinessWeek, and Shanghai Education. He has also written for Hong Kong's English and Chinese language press. He has also briefed the office of the US Secretary of Education and is a member of the National Committee on US–China Relations.

Prof. Jozef Ritzen a Dutch national, trained as a physics engineer (Delft University of Technology) and an economist (Erasmus University Rotterdam, Ph.D., cum laude) and has held professorial appointments with Nijmegen University and Erasmus University in The Netherlands, the University of California-Berkeley and the Robert M. LaFollette Institute of Public Affairs at the University of Wisconsin-Madison in the USA.

He was Minister of Education, Culture, and Science of The Netherlands from 1989 to 1998, one of the longest serving Ministers of Education in the world. During his term, he enacted a series of major reforms throughout the Dutch education system. Subsequently, he served as Vice President of the World Bank's Human Development Network and as President of Maastricht University.

He has written or co-authored fourteen books and many articles (often co-authored) in the fields of education, economics, public finance, and development economics. His latest book is: *A Second Change for Europe* (Springer, 2017).

He has also made significant contributions to agencies such as the World Bank, UNESCO, and OECD, especially in the field of education, economic growth, and social cohesion.

He is now honorary professor of Maastricht University and UNU/Merit, a member of the International Advisory Boards of the University of Siegen (Germany), the Charles University in Prague (Czech Republic) and King Abdulaziz University (Jeddah, Saudi Arabia), adviser to several ministers of education, Chair and Founder of Empower European Universities, and Initiator of the Vibrant Europe Forum which wants to contribute to European Policy Development. Professor Ritzen is a member of the KAU IAB.

Prof. Guaning Su was the second president of Nanyang Technological University (NTU) Singapore from 2003 to 2011 and is a tenured professor of electrical and electronic engineering. He holds a B.Sc. in Electrical Engineering (1971), a M.S.E.E. (1972) from the California Institute of Technology, a M.S. (Statistics) (1982), and a Ph.D. (Electrical Engineering) (1983) from Stanford University as well as an Honorary Doctor of Science (2015) from the University of Alberta. He joined the newly formed research and development arm of the Ministry of Defence Singapore in 1972 and headed the Defence Science Organisation (DSO, later to become DSO National Laboratories) from 1986 to 1997. He was Deputy Secretary (Technology) at the Ministry of Defence, Singapore from 1998 to 2001 and Founding Chief Executive, Defence Science and Technology Agency (DSTA) from 2000 to 2002. He joined Nanyang Technological University in 2002 as president-designate and was inaugurated as the second president in 2003.

Professor Su's presidency coincided with major changes of university governance in Singapore. Seizing those opportunities, he built three new schools, doubled the enrollment, multiplied competitive research funding sevenfold and transformed NTU from a narrowly focused teaching university into a technology and innovation powerhouse. World rankings rose to 12th in the world in 2018. He is currently Chairman of the International Advisory Board (IAB) of the Hong Kong Polytechnic University and a member of the IAB of King Abdulaziz University, Saudi Arabia.

Professor Su was conferred the National Science and Technology Medal and the Meritorious Service Medal by Singapore, Knighthood of the Legion of Honour by France, and the Friendship Award by China. He is a Life Fellow of IEEE and Fellow of the Singapore Academy of Engineering. Professor Su is a member of the KAU IAB.

Part I
Implementation of Global Partnerships

King Abdulaziz University's Approach to International Collaboration

Abdulrahman Al-Youbi and Adnan H. M. Zahed

1 Introduction

This section first explains the differences between the terms "cooperation," "collaboration," and "partnership," which are used interchangeably in the literature. It then highlights the reasons King Abdulaziz University (KAU) that has chosen to collaborate with other academic and research institutes.

1.1 Definition of Cooperation, Collaboration, and Partnership

Cooperative work is accomplished by dividing a task among participants where each is responsible for a portion of it [1]. Cooperation is achieved if all participants do their assigned parts and send them back to the work coordinator. Cooperative bodies have specific and joint rights and responsibilities. Each cooperative body has an equal share of the risk as well as the reward. The concept of "international cooperation" describes cooperative activities between two or more countries. The policies of the participating partners are negotiated to bring agreements more in line with each side's preferences. Once policies become more compatible, the act of cooperation is completed [2, 3].

The term "collaboration" is the action of working together with others to produce or create something, and in the context of academic bodies, it is used mostly on the level of research. In other words, it is the mutual engagement of participants in a coordinated effort to solve a problem together [4]. However, the collaboration also involves cooperation, in which the responsibilities of each partner may not be shared equally.

Partnership is a co-term used in cooperation as well as collaboration to indicate that two or more partners are cooperating to conduct the task. Partnerships may be between researchers in the same laboratory or academic department, between researchers from different departments in the same institution, or even between researchers in different institutions or different countries. The latter case may be sometimes complicated due to cultural differences.

The three terms are used interchangeably, although they represent different ways of contributing to a group. Cooperation can be achieved if all participants do their assigned parts separately and bring their results to the table, while the collaboration implies direct interaction among the partners to reach the desired result. This interaction often involves negotiations, discussions, and consideration of different perspectives. In other words, cooperation focuses on working together to create an end product, while participants in collaboration share in the process of knowledge creation [5]. Therefore, the collaboration is appropriate for complex projects involving multiple teams or agencies, while the cooperation is suitable for projects in which each participant is responsible for performing a certain segment of the complete task. In both cases, partnership also frequently occurs.

It is to be mentioned here that the opposite of cooperation or collaboration is "competition." A small amount of competition is effective in encouraging different organizations to seek a better position, but excessive levels of competition have negative consequences. Many institutions cooperate in research and collaborate in the research and joint degrees, but still see each other as "competitors" as they try to attract the best students and staff and to get higher rankings.

1.2 King Abdulaziz University's Choice to Pursue Collaboration

King Abdulaziz University (KAU) realized early on the importance of international university cooperation and collaboration to expedite its way toward becoming a world-class university. As a result, it has established joint

A. Al-Youbi · A. H. M. Zahed (✉)
King Abdulaziz University, Jeddah, Saudi Arabia
e-mail: azahed@kau.edu.sa

© The Author(s) 2020
A. Al-Youbi et al. (eds.), *Successful Global Collaborations in Higher Education Institutions*,
https://doi.org/10.1007/978-3-030-25525-1_1

international cooperation agreements and service contracts with many of the world's distinguished universities and educational institutions. It has also established the Distinctive Scientists Program to create collaboration programs between KAU researchers and well-known researchers from all over the globe. These steps, along with other accomplishments, have accelerated the achievement of KAU's objective to increase its ranking and become a world-class university.

2 International Collaboration

International cooperation and collaboration are modes of working together to attain the best results in the development of solutions to international problems. Modern life has brought luxury to human beings, but at the same time, it has created many massive problems such as global warming, an extreme need for energy, excessive demand for water, crowded cities, the rapid aging of people, and a high occurrence of natural disasters. These huge problems necessitate collaboration between universities and industry worldwide to bridge the gap between knowledge and innovation.

A comprehensive paper by Ankrah and Al-Tabbaa [6] on universities–industry collaboration (UIC) for the period from 1990–2014 studied the different organizational forms of UIC, motivations at universities and in industry for UIC, the process of forming UICs, activities undertaken in UICs, the factors facilitating or impeding UICs, and the benefits from UICs for both the universities and the industry. The paper explains that collaboration between universities and industry is increasingly perceived as a vehicle to enhancing innovation through knowledge exchange. This is evident from the significant increase in studies that investigate the topic from different perspectives.

The academia–industry collaboration in science and technology-based innovation has resulted in role sharing between universities and companies resulting in global problem solving with an emphasis on human resources development.

International cooperation and collaboration are carried out between partners working traditionally together in the same field or collaboratively in various fields in order to find an optimized solution or to introduce a non-traditional or creative solution for an international problem. The climate problem, growing energy consumption, high rates of fatal car accidents, global peace, and fighting terrorism and crime are the most famous examples of widespread global problems. To find the best scientific and applicable solutions to such problems requires the strengthening of cooperation/ collaboration between universities, research institutions, civil societies, and industrial sectors. At times, international

policies have a key role to play in developing appropriate solutions and preparing them for implementation.

The following section, Sect. 3, deals with how international collaboration is implemented by higher education institutions, while Sect. 4 explains the importance of international collaboration for universities.

3 International Collaboration and Cooperation Among Universities

International university collaboration is a part of the much wider arena of international collaboration. The topic of international university collaboration has been prominent in recent times and has become a significant and important university activity [7]. In recent years, universities have managed to include international cooperation and collaboration as integral elements of their missions and functions although it is a laborious process. This cooperation and collaboration are forms of working together to attain the best results in learning, training, and research.

University cooperation has recently been successfully incorporated into the institutional structure of an increasing number of universities. Most universities currently have an office or administration in charge of international university cooperation, with a definite strategy and an action plan to carry out a series of international activities. In recent years, rising expectations have been generated with regard to the need to adopt new perspectives in international university cooperation. University authorities have to overcome budgetary constraints and other impediments in order to pursue the necessary efforts to enhance the incorporation of international cooperation in their institutions.

For a long time, education and scientific research have been focused on a lot in international cooperation/ collaboration. Therefore, universities and research institutions are called upon to promote cooperation in order to develop knowledge, which will benefit all humankind [7]. Recently, introducing international collaboration as one of the university strategic objectives has opened new paths for the exchange of academic expertise, saving effort and money and achieving qualitative leaps in strengthening systems management and development.

Technical international cooperation is another form of international university cooperation. It includes activities whose primary aim is to increase the level of knowledge, technology, practical know-how or productive attitudes of the population, that is to say, to increase their reserve of human intellectual capital or their ability to use their current resources with greater efficiency [8]. The basic aim of technical cooperation is to support the ability of people and organizations in creating, adapting, strengthening, and sustaining their capacity to set their own objectives. Its aims are that institutions with a more advanced level of development in certain areas would contribute to the solution of specific problems of less developed institutions through the transference and interchange of scientific and technological capacity and human and material resources.

Technical cooperation is often associated with actions intended to strengthen individual and organizational capacity by offering a wide range of technical opportunities to its beneficiaries. Technical cooperation can be strengthened via improving the following cooperative channels:

- Educational cooperation: student exchange, teacher exchange, language learning, joint degrees, and curricula developments
- Research cooperation: joint research activities
- Training cooperation: training programs and supplying training equipment and materials
- Cultural cooperation: social and cultural programs
- Scholarships
- Strategic partnerships.

4 The Importance of International Collaboration for Universities

International partnerships between universities are beneficial to all, including staff and students. Forming links with other universities has become highly necessary and is easily managed. Universities across the world are seeking to form global partnerships and foster relationships with other institutions. This helps student recruitment in two main ways: For domestic students, it offers the opportunity to travel internationally via student exchange programs, and vice versa for students at partnered universities. It also enables universities to better understand the culture of other nations [9]. Additionally, international collaboration programs help by providing students with the ability to study, work, and travel worldwide.

Partnerships with highly ranked international universities provide greater opportunities for cultural exchange and the development of academic systems, which in turn will positively reflect on the development of various academic and research university sectors. Developing the abilities and skills of human resources from student to professor is the most significant factor in the strategic development process. For these benefits, universities all over the world seek to create international partnerships with similar universities and academic institutions. Academic exchange programs, including international visits, enable students and staff members on both sides to learn about each other's culture. Such programs also promote intercultural skills in a globalized world, help people to work effectively in a new environment, open new channels for academic cooperation, and help people to make new friendships. This has a direct effect on university development processes and the quality of academic and research programs.

Significantly, it is known that one in five of the world's scientific papers is co-authored internationally. As a result of the expansion of communication methods, academics and researchers are finding it easier to collaborate with their foreign counterparts, and the exchange of academic ideas has become much simpler to organize.

The ability to scrutinize, debate, and share experience is essential for academic and scientific accomplishment. International collaborations help to facilitate this. In terms of teaching, benefits include curriculum development and degrees formed in collaboration with partner institutions. However, developing successful relationships takes a long time and requires understanding the culture and goals of each other's institutions in order to ensure compatibility in terms of ethics and standards. Therefore, the most important aspect of a partnership's endurance is an alliance of ideas and goals. This means selecting carefully institutions to partner with and confirming at every stage that all members of the partnership are on the same page [9].

5 International Collaboration in Higher Education in Saudi Arabia

International cooperation in higher education in Saudi Arabia is a part of the strategic goal of the Ministry of Education (MOE). It aims to develop, improve, enhance, and raise the level of higher education in the country through cooperation with distinguished international higher education and research institutions. This is achieved via signing agreements and alliances and by building international partnerships in academic and research areas [10]. The MOE has established the "General Administration for International Cooperation" within its administrative structure. The unit was established because of the Ministry's belief in the importance of international cooperation mechanisms in education and their strong effects on fostering globalization, massification, and marketization of higher education.

The objective of the General Administration of International Cooperation is to ensure effective mutually beneficial coordination with universities and academic research agencies outside the kingdom. It has an important role in building bridges of knowledge between Saudi universities and

Fig. 1 Administration of international agreements at KAU

internationally prestigious and distinguished higher educational institutions. It seeks to promote knowledge and cultural exchange through the expansion of scholarships. It coordinates training programs, seminars, conferences, and international exhibitions, and it raises the level of performance and development of international cooperation in various fields of knowledge. The administration is eager to contribute to, highlight and reinforce Saudi Arabia's general development in the field of higher education. The MOE and the Saudi universities have signed a number of memorandums of cooperation and service contracts with ministries and prestigious universities around the globe.

6 International Collaboration at King Abdulaziz University

This section discusses the international collaborations at King Abdulaziz University (KAU).

6.1 KAU Administration of International Agreements

At KAU, there is an "Administration of International Agreements" that organizes, follows up, and develops international agreements between KAU and international universities and research centers. The aim is to accelerate scientific progress and expedite technology transfer from the world's most prestigious universities and scientific institutes to KAU. The administration prepares a fully automated management system of international agreements and service contracts and ensures that adequate budgetary provisions are in place for effective task design and implementation. It also edits a final statistical analysis report detailing the achievements of the various agreements.

The structure of the administration is illustrated in Fig. 1. It consists of five units under the management of a general supervisor who reports directly to the KAU President. However, to ensure administrative effectiveness, the University Vice Presidents monitor and supervise the five units according to their fields of responsibility. The Research Agreements Unit is under the supervision of the Vice President for Graduate Studies and Scientific Research, while the Educational Agreements Unit is under the supervision of the Vice President for Academic Affairs. The Creative and Innovative Agreements Unit is under the supervision of the Vice President for Business and Knowledge Creativity, while the Administrative and Training Agreements Unit is under the supervision of both the Vice President and the Vice President for Development. And finally, the Academic Accreditation and Classification Agreements Unit is under the supervision of the Vice President for Development.

6.2 Agreements with Leading Universities

King Abdulaziz University has made joint international cooperation agreements and service contracts with many of the world's top universities and educational institutions. There are currently more than 77 operational service contracts and several other agreements and memorandums of understanding between KAU and universities, scientific institutions, and specialized companies in many countries such as the USA, Canada, and Argentina in the Americas; the UK, France, Spain, Germany, Finland, Switzerland,

Austria, the Netherlands, Belgium and Turkey in Europe; China, South Korea, Japan, Singapore and Malaysia in Asia; and Australia and New Zealand in the South Pacific. These agreements and service contracts specialize in the implementation of joint research projects and patents; the exchange of students, staff, faculty members, and scientific expertise; the establishment of joint graduate programs; curriculum development; the development of distance education; training programs for medical, engineering, and maritime studies graduate students; and training for faculty members.

6.3 International Students Program

The international graduate students program started some years ago and is successfully attracting students from different countries. KAU grants scholarships to talented international students to pursue their studies in its various university graduate programs. KAU admits top international students in its graduate programs. Currently, KAU has 193 graduate programs in all of its specializations, divided into Ph.D. (43), Master's degree (143), and Higher Diploma (7). Recently, the number of new entrants has increased significantly, and this growth has necessitated strengthening and invigorating all aspects of higher educational academic research at KAU. This has helped to ensure that when KAU graduates enter the employment market, their competencies and qualifications are sought after and welcomed by international employers. KAU has become a recognized venue for "elite higher education." It has a reputation for academic excellence and is considered to represent quality higher education. These factors enable KAU to have the privilege of receiving high levels of funding and to recruit the most academically talented international students.

6.4 Distinguished Scientist Program

The 9th Development Plan of the Kingdom of Saudi Arabia states that it will concentrate on scientific research and attract scientists of high caliber to work in universities and research centers. The 2005–2030 Plan of Higher Education in Saudi Arabia (AAFAQ Plan) states that universities should attract the best scientists, while the KAU Strategic Plan states that it will be transformed into a Research University. The International Advisory Board (IAB) of KAU suggested in its second meeting (July 2011) that KAU should attract internationally distinguished scientists to enhance its research quality. Accordingly, in June 2011, KAU started an ambitious program to employ distinguished scientists. Colleges, Research Groups, and Centers search for distinguished scientists whose specialization fits the research areas and send

their selection to a KAU committee which starts writing to the selected distinguished scientists inviting them to visit KAU and meet with the local scientists to discuss possible types of collaboration. At the end of the visit, a decision is taken as to whether to go ahead with the collaboration or not. Many distinguished scientists have preferred to work part-time, while a few have moved to KAU.

The duties of the distinguished scientists can be summarized as follows: to write research proposals with KAU researchers to the KAU Deanship of Scientific Research and to the King Abdulaziz City of Science and Technology (KACST), especially for the National Strategic Research Program; to collaborate with and guide the local academic staff to conduct the research; to co-supervise graduate students; to examine graduate students theses; to give seminars, lectures, and short courses; to co-author books; to participate in establishing business incubators; to participate in the councils of the centers of research excellence; to help KAU graduates to get admission in graduate programs at universities abroad; and to help KAU academic staff get acceptance for Sabbatical years in their home universities.

The outcome of the program may be summarized in the following points: Numerous research proposals have been submitted to the KAU Deanship of Scientific Research by distinguished scientists in collaboration with more than 150 KAU academic staff; numerous research proposals have been submitted to King Abdulaziz City for Science and Technology (KACST); various scientific books have been published; four international scientific journals have been launched: Bulletin of Mathematical Sciences (published by Springer), The Journal of Microscopy and Ultrastructure (published by Elsevier), Genomic Medicine (published by Nature Partner Journals, NPJ), and Climate and Atmospheric Science (published by Nature Partner Journals, NPJ).

6.5 International Advisory Board (IAB)

King Abdulaziz University (KAU) has undertaken genuine transformational steps to establish partnerships and cooperative programs with international educational and industrial institutions in order to enhance and improve its academic and educational profile and status. To achieve a substantive leap forward in quality in levels of performance in educational, academic research, and community services, in 2010, KAU established an International Advisory Board (IAB). It is benefiting from the experience of international pioneers in the industry and higher education who have made significant contributions to the development of higher education worldwide. The aim of the IAB has been to provide KAU with diverse input and guidance from the international community in order to support its quest for academic and educational excellence and ultimately, its international recognition. To ensure that KAU receives a diversity of ideas and views, the IAB represents a variety of disciplines and an extensive range of backgrounds.

The main objectives of the IAB are: to participate in re-formulating KAU's strategic plans; to achieve its goals in the educational process, scientific research, and community service; to enable the university to surpass and accomplish distinction in knowledge accumulation, science, and technology; to enhance the university's status and international profile, especially in the fields of research and innovation; to contribute to the formation of strategic alliances between KAU and different sectors in the Saudi community, as well as international institutions; to establish and activate partnerships with international universities and research centers; and to provide consultancy to KAU as well as to other Saudi institutions wishing to take advantage of the expertise, experience, and qualifications of IAB members [11].

6.6 Research Groups

KAU initiated the idea of forming research groups to enhance cooperation between researchers from different specializations. Each group consists of up to 15 researchers and academics (of all ranks including fresh academics and graduate students) under the leadership of one prominent scientist. The group must include one collaborating scientist from an international university. Each research group has a main broad specialization that is different from the specializations of other groups. The research proposals submitted by research groups are prioritized in terms of funding over proposals submitted by individuals. To date, twenty-five research groups have been formed covering a wide spectrum of specializations. These are the: Saudi Diabetes Research Group; Oral and Dental Diseases Research Group; Renewable Energy Group; Software Engineering and Distributed Systems Group; Economic and Market Research Group; Nonlinear Analysis and Applied Mathematics Group; Biotechnology Group; Engineering Management and Quality Improvement Group; Information Security Research Group; Advances in Composites, Synthesis and Applications Group; Clinical Nutrition Group; Communication Systems and Networks Group; Plant Biology Group; Laser Applications Group; Diagnostic and Therapeutic Engineering Group; Modeling and Simulation of Complex Systems Group; Bioactive Natural Products Group; Medicinal Plants Group; Lithography in Device Fabrication and Development Group; Metal Oxides Research Group; Carbon Nanostructures Group; Vitamin D Pharmacogenomics Group; Virtual Reality Research Group; Sustainable Green Chemistry Group; and Sleep Disorder Research Group.

In addition to publishing papers in ISI ranked journals, the research groups are committed to working on projects that benefit the local community as well as the national Saudi community.

6.7 KAU–Industry Collaboration

Collaboration between KAU and industry is managed by the Research and Consulting Institute (RACI). RACI is a consultation center which provides its services in research and development on a contractual basis with the utmost flexibility and professionalism to suit both the public as well as the private sectors. RACI is one of the most important investment arms of KAU. It offers a number of services including: contractual research, consultancy, project management, educational services, and training. In addition, RACI manages KAU's scientific chairs and central laboratories.

The objectives of RACI are to have a strong partnership with the society based on KAU's responsibility toward the country and its citizens; to have a modern methodology for providing consultation experiences that meet international standards; and to market KAU human and technical abilities via professional and competitive ways.

The capabilities of RACI include: a strong relationship with effective players in the consulting service industry; access to more than 5000 researchers from various specialties at KAU to perform services offered by RACI such as contractual research, consultations, training, and educational services; more than 50 central laboratories at medicine, engineering, computing, science, and business schools, which can provide different services to both the public and the private sectors; and more than 200 active expert houses that offer consulting services to various sectors in the kingdom. These expert houses cover most of the fields including medicine, engineering, computing, science, economics, and business.

6.8 Knowledge and Business Alliance

In addition to the Research and Consulting Institute, KAU and the public and private sectors also collaborate through the Knowledge and Business Alliance (K&B). As the largest and one of the most prominent universities in Saudi Arabia, KAU has a proven record in providing research solutions. KAU has at its disposal about 50 years' worth of "know-how" and organizational knowledge competence, in addition to a magnitude of other resources and assets including: rich expertise and established industry leadership; state-of-the-art research infrastructures; and a stimulating working environment. KAU clients and partners are diverse, ranging from entrepreneurs to developers, from locals to internationals, and from visitors to tenants. However, they have one aspect in common: They are empowered through the synergy of KAU knowledge partners. K&B facilitates the creation of these knowledge networks through its four main divisions:

(1) Expert Houses Sector: Drawing on KAU's powerful knowledge base of varied specializations and highly qualified academic personnel, these are university-supervised, faculty-operated establishments that offer specialized consulting services to both private and public sectors.
(2) Central Laboratories Sector: These laboratories provide a powerful combination of expertise, competent staff, and state-of-the-art equipment dedicated to providing specialized and advanced laboratory consultations and workshop services, including standardized procedures, certified tests, and analytical studies.
(3) Business Incubators Sector: This sector offers valuable support services and resources to KAU students and graduates with promising and innovative business ideas and projects. Moreover, it helps entrepreneurial firms survive and grow during vulnerable start-up phases.
(4) Knowledge Parks Sector: These parks provide a smart and stimulating working environment which enables tenants to reduce their cost of operation and to enhance their competitiveness through privileged access to KAU's professors, students, labs, cutting-edge technological infrastructure, and a wealth of other supporting services.

6.9 Wadi Jeddah (Jeddah Valley) Company

Another channel for collaboration with industry is the Wadi Jeddah Company. It is wholly owned by KAU and represents KAU's investment arm. It operates on a commercial basis in the process of investment and profitability and contributes to the development of the knowledge economy. To achieve its goals, Wadi Jeddah has established five companies so far. These are:

(1) Molecular Imaging Center: This was established due to the increasing need for a specialized center in cancer diagnosis as well as in the production of the radioactive materials needed in the diagnosis. The company has partnered with the General Electric Company to operate the project.
(2) Manarat Al-Ma'arefa (Knowledge Minarets): This was established for knowledge transfer and R&D. It works on creating a suitable environment to attract scholars and businesspeople.

(3) Saudi Alliance for Development of Education and Training (SAFEA): This project is implemented through a partnership contract with the Finnish company, EduCluster, which comes under the University of Jyväskylä, one of the largest universities in Finland known for its multidisciplinary activities in creativity and innovation in the field of education and research.
(4) Medical Knowledge Village: This company plans to build a hospital and a hotel of international standard on the Obhur Campus (North Jeddah) of KAU.
(5) Clinical Research Organization: This medical research company is to be a model center for conducting clinical research on drugs. It plans to establish partnerships with international pharmaceutical companies.

7 Outcomes of Collaboration at King Abdulaziz University

King Abdulaziz University constitutes a rich source of graduates and skilled cadres which can help address the needs of the country and contribute to its development. To achieve its objectives and become one of the top universities in the world, KAU adopts a clear vision, responds accordingly to changing community needs and circumstances, provides a congenial academic environment, and establishes cultural cooperation with international universities. This results in the university having outstanding educational programs, skilled graduates, rich scientific research, and the ability to make effective contributions to society. The need for excellence in international relations is triggered by the diversity of the university's departments and the importance of coordinating collaboration and cooperation with other universities.

The KAU Vision regarding international cooperation is to establish internationally effective partnerships to support the university's vision, while its message is to participate in the development of the university into a leading international, cultural, scientific, and research collaboration.

The achievements of the international agreements held between King Abdulaziz University and world-class universities have resulted in eighty-one agreements in various fields. The total budget of these agreements has amounted to more than US $120 million. The achievements include: publishing numerous scientific papers in ISI journals and specialized international conferences; registering numerous patents at international organizations; implementing 1400 training, development or technology transfer programs; developing graduate programs; and developing student and professor exchange programs.

8 Conclusion

International university cooperation is a must, especially for university students and professors in the early stages of their careers. International cooperation and collaboration should be an integral element of the university mission and functions. This is achieved by universities when they assume responsibility for cooperating with other world-class institutions. International university collaboration and cooperation can take place in many avenues of university work: education, research, training, culture cooperation, and scholarships.

Research cooperation among individuals is no longer complicated, even though these researchers work at institutions in different countries and have cultural differences. Modern communication methods have facilitated the research projects they conduct. Globally, student exchange is increasing, and the total number of Saudi students studying abroad has also grown rapidly in recent years, largely funded by the Saudi government scholarship programs. International student and staff exchange increases the concerned individuals' capacity for self-reflection, self-reliance, and self-confidence. Such exchanges also help individuals develop more mature and objective perceptions concerning their home and foreign countries, thereby contributing to international tranquility by enhancing multicultural understanding. Such an exchange also crucially promotes creative thinking.

International collaboration and cooperation in higher education is a strategic goal of the Saudi Ministry of Education. In line with this goal, the MOE is actively involved in building bridges of knowledge between Saudi universities and world distinguished educational institutions to promote knowledge and cultural exchange. Each Saudi university, including King Abdulaziz University, has established joint international cooperation agreements and service contracts with many of the world's top-ranking distinguished universities and educational institutions. The international strategic policy of world-class universities is intended to improve education, strengthen both external and internal collaboration, build research partnerships with other world-class universities, and attract highly talented students and professors from around the world. Success in so doing provides a diversity of academic environments and scientific approaches and is a mark of distinction and strength.

Any world-class university endeavors to develop its leading position by providing researchers and students with excellent opportunities for cooperation, collaboration, and exchange with other national and international universities. Successful implementation of this strategy enables the university's researchers and students to participate in international research and research-based teaching to acquire a truly global outlook. Such a strategy can be implemented by means of research projects, student symposia, summer programs, workshops, conferences, and congresses. Scholarship grants and programs, such as the "International Students Program" of KAU promote mutual understanding between individuals and institutions in the global arena. Such mutual and mutually beneficial understanding can be accomplished through the educational and cultural exchange of students, knowledge, and skills and is of crucial significance to mankind's aspirations to live in harmony and peace.

Other cooperative programs provide opportunities for study, lecturing, curricular development, postdoctoral research, advanced joint research grants, visits, and aid in promoting mutual cultural understanding. Such programs also assist in the internationalization of campuses, curricula, and communities. Grant programs facilitate an international educational and cultural exchange for students, teachers, professionals, and scientists. This exchange is accomplished through direct interactions of individuals who are able to live and work together in order to learn from host country inhabitants in a daily sharing of mutually enriching cultural experiences.

King Abdulaziz University realized early on the importance of international university cooperation and collaboration to expedite its way toward becoming a world-class university. The impact of this on KAU has strengthened its scientific research and higher education sector (international students), improved the quality of its academic programs, and facilitated the administrative development and restructuring of KAU through its successive strategic plans. International collaboration has achieved alignment between KAU's vision and objectives and the programs of the Kingdom of Saudi Arabia Vision 2030. Enhancing the ranking of KAU is an outcome of the development plans and activities based on international collaboration.

And finally, it is worth mentioning that although some other Saudi universities have similar programs of collaboration, none of them have all the programs of KAU. It is no wonder that KAU is ranked as the top Saudi university in the list of world university rankings (Shanghai, Times, and QS). KAU was declared by the Times Higher Education ranking to be the top university in the MENA region for two successive years (2017 and 2018).

Acknowledgements The authors of this chapter would like to thank Prof. Mahmoud Nadim Nahas and Prof. Ahmad Hegazy for collecting the data needed for the manuscript.

References

1. Roschelle, J., & Teasley, S. (1995). The construction of shared knowledge in collaborative problem solving. In C. E. O'Malley (Ed.), *Computer supported collaborative learning* (pp. 69–97). Heidelberg: Springer.
2. Keohane, R. (1984). *After hegemony: Cooperation and discord in the world political economy*. Princeton: Princeton University Press.
3. Gonzales-Tablas, M. A. (1995). *Visión Global de la Cooperación para el Desarrollo*. Barcelona: Icaria Editorial.
4. Dillenbourg, P., Baker, M., Blaye, A., & O'Malley, C. (1996). The evolution of research on collaborative learning. In E. Spada & P. Reiman (Eds.), *Humans and machine: Towards an interdisciplinary learning science* (pp. 189–211). Oxford: Elsevier.
5. Kozar, O. (2010). Towards better group work: Seeing the difference between cooperation and collaboration. *English Teaching Forum, 48*(2), 16–23.
6. Ankra, S., & Al-Tabbaa, O. (2015). Universities-industry collaboration: A systematic review. *Scandinavian Journal of Management, 31*(3), 387–408. https://doi.org/10.1016/j.scaman.2015.02.003.
7. Development Cooperation Directorate. Website, Organization for Economic Cooperation and Development (OECD). http://www.oecd.org/dac. Accessed March 30, 2019.
8. Technical cooperation for capacity development. Perspectives note, OECD/DAC Report, 2011. http://www.oecd.org/dac/governance-development/48260262.pdf. Accessed March 30, 2019.
9. QS Digital Marketing. Why are international collaborations so important for universities? http://www.qs.com/why-are-international-collaborations-so-important-for-universities/. Accessed March 30, 2019.
10. Saudi Ministry of Education. https://departments.moe.gov.sa/InternationalCooperation/Pages/default.aspx. Accessed March 30, 2019.
11. Tayeb, O., Zahed, A., & Ritzen, J. (Eds.). (2016). *Becoming a world-class university: The case of King Abdulaziz University*. Cham, Switzerland: Springer.

Open Access This chapter is licensed under the terms of the Creative Commons Attribution 4.0 International License (http://creativecommons.org/licenses/by/4.0/), which permits use, sharing, adaptation, distribution and reproduction in any medium or format, as long as you give appropriate credit to the original author(s) and the source, provide a link to the Creative Commons license and indicate if changes were made.

The images or other third party material in this chapter are included in the chapter's Creative Commons license, unless indicated otherwise in a credit line to the material. If material is not included in the chapter's Creative Commons license and your intended use is not permitted by statutory regulation or exceeds the permitted use, you will need to obtain permission directly from the copyright holder.

Creating an Organizational Climate for Global Partnerships: Challenges and Opportunities

2

William G. Tierney

1 Introduction

All too often, observers of tertiary education assume that the way the academic world functions today is the way it always has been organized. And yet, colleges and universities always have been in a state of change. If "world-class rankings" had been compiled in the late nineteenth century, no institutions in the USA would have likely made the list. In the most recent Shanghai Jiao Tong Rankings of World Universities, however, American universities held most of the top 20 positions, and over 50 of the top 100 spots [1].

With this constant state of flux in the academic world, the institutions that are most successful are those which are able to manage change and innovation in a world defined by globalization. Those who adhere to a principle of "staying the course" are likely to run aground, due to the rapidly changing conditions of the larger environment. Globalization highlights the necessity for institutions to be outward looking rather than insular. The ecology of global institutions is one where partnerships and alliances are created and maintained as opposed to a "go it alone" strategy where institutions fail or succeed by their own initiative [2].

My purpose here is to outline what the conditions are for an organization to create global partnerships and how to sustain them. As I shall elaborate, an innovative organization is different from a stable one. It requires different skills from its participants, and it functions in a different way than a stable organization. Global partnerships demand an innovative climate—but such an undertaking is not without risks and challenges.

Accordingly, I begin with an overview of how I conceive of an organization's culture, in general, and universities, in particular. I then consider the environment in which universities currently exist as framed by globalization, and subsequently turn to a discussion of how an innovative culture might be established and maintained to enable global partnerships to be implemented and to succeed.

2 Defining Organizational Culture

Our lack of understanding about the role of organizational culture in improving management and institutional performance inhibits our ability to address the challenges that face higher education and confounds our ability to create and maintain global partnerships. Colleges and universities face increasing complexity and fragmentation [3]. As decision-making contexts grow more obscure, costs increase, and resources become more difficult to allocate, leaders in higher education benefit from understanding their institutions as cultural entities. They need to recognize that those with whom they will work on a global partnership will have a culture different from their own. The point is certainly not that one organizational culture is better than another, but instead, that working across cultural boundaries is necessary for any leader involved in global partnerships [4].

As before, these leaders continue to make difficult decisions. These decisions, however, need not engender the degree of conflict that they usually have prompted. Indeed, properly informed by an awareness of culture, tough decisions may contribute to an institution's sense of purpose and identity and will facilitate the ability to create and maintain global partnerships. Moreover, to implement decisions, leaders must have a full, nuanced understanding of the organization's culture. Only then can they articulate decisions in a way that will speak to the needs of various constituencies and marshal their support. Without an understanding of one's own culture, the ability to create connections with another organization's culture becomes that much more difficult [5].

Cultural influences occur at many levels, within the department and the institution, as well as between universities when they work with one another, regardless of

W. G. Tierney (✉)
University of Southern California, Los Angeles, USA
e-mail: wgtiern@usc.edu

© The Author(s) 2020
A. Al-Youbi et al. (eds.), *Successful Global Collaborations in Higher Education Institutions*,
https://doi.org/10.1007/978-3-030-25525-1_2

whether the companion organization is in the same country or abroad. Because these cultures vary dramatically, a central goal of understanding organizational culture is to minimize the occurrence and consequences of cultural conflict and help foster the development of shared goals. Studying the cultural dynamics of educational institutions and systems equips us to understand and, hopefully, reduce adversarial relationships. Equally important, it will enable us to recognize how those actions and shared goals are most likely to succeed and how they can best be implemented.

One assumption of this chapter is that more often than not, more than one choice exists for the decision-maker; one simple answer most often does not exist. No matter how much information we gather, frequently we are able to choose from several viable alternatives. Culture influences the decision. Effective administrators are well aware that they can take a given action in some institutions but not in others. They are less aware of why this is true. Bringing the dimensions and dynamics of culture to consciousness helps leaders assess the reasons for such differences in institutional responsiveness and performance. This will allow them to evaluate likely consequences before, not after, they act. An understanding of the cultural determinants of an organization enables a decision-maker not only to understand their organization, but also those with whom they will enter into a global partnership [6].

It is important to reiterate that an understanding of organizational culture is not a panacea to all administrative problems, or a certainty that global partnerships will always be successful. An understanding of culture, for example, will not automatically increase enrollments, increase research grants, or increase the number of global partnerships that get formed. However, an administrator's correct interpretation of the organization's culture can provide critical insight about which of the many possible avenues to choose from is best when deciding about how to increase enrollment, whether to undertake a particular approach to increasing research output, or how to improve global partnerships. Indeed, the most persuasive case for studying organizational culture is quite simply that we no longer need to tolerate the consequences of our ignorance, nor, for that matter, will a rapidly changing environment permit us to do so. By advocating for a broad perspective, organizational culture encourages practitioners to:

- consider real or potential conflicts not in isolation but on the broad canvas of organizational life
- recognize structural or operational contradictions that suggest tensions in the organization
- implement and evaluate everyday decisions with a keen awareness of their role in and influence upon organizational culture

- understand the symbolic dimensions of ostensibly instrumental decisions and actions
- consider why different groups in the organization hold varying perceptions about institutional performance.

Many administrators intuitively understand that organizational culture is important; their actions sometimes reflect the points mentioned above. A framework for organizational culture provides administrators with the capability to better articulate and address this crucial foundation for improving organizational performance in general, and global partnerships in particular.

When anthropologists conduct fieldwork to better understand the culture of a society or a collective group, they are equipped with disciplinary-specific terms, such as "fictive kinship," that define commonly encountered phenomena. These terms are not only intelligible to other anthropologists, but they are deemed crucial for a thorough description and analysis of a given culture or cultural activity. For an understanding of institutional culture in higher education, it is therefore useful to pinpoint similarly important phenomena and provide a working terminology that can serve as the basis for a conceptual framework. Six such terms define an organization's culture at a university: mission, socialization, information, strategy, leadership, and environment [7]. In what follows, I provide a thumbnail definition of these terms in relation to how to think about global partnerships.

- *Mission*: A mission is succinct, clear, and orients the institution to its primary roles in society. If global partnerships are a central part of a university's role, then one expects to see mention of international outreach and involvement.
- *Socialization*: Socialization pertains to how new members are oriented to the mission and functions of the institution. Socialization is not a static concept and changes and adapts as individuals enter and exit the organization. If global outreach is important, then individuals will be socialized in a manner that enables them to learn about more than their discipline, country, or institution.
- *Information*: The material that individuals receive and the manner in which it is conveyed pertains to this term. If the organization honors global partnerships, then a significant communicative symbol pertains to all of the members receiving information and updates about international engagements.
- *Strategy*: Any organization will have an implicit or explicit plan about the direction the organization is taking; if global partnerships are important then it will be one key component of a university's strategic plan.

- *Leadership*: The board, university president, and senior administrators are obvious actors who are key in the direction the university will take. Global partnerships should have someone who oversees the strategic direction the university takes as a member of the senior leadership team.
- *Environment*: A university has a variety of geographies that it can define as its sphere of influence. A local institution may define nothing more than the city or town where it is located. Regional universities may have a broader geographic region but define their clientele and outreach as a region within the country. A university that desires long-standing and impactful global partnerships will see its environment in much broader terms. Nevertheless, a university need not be so broad as defining "the world" as its environment. Instead, for strategic reasons, the institution may focus on one particular area such as the Mideast or Africa. By focusing in this manner, the organization helps frame what is and is not of importance to the university's members.

3 Defining Globalization

The rapid development and adoption of technology along with more open economies have created an integrated global economy [8]. The globalization process has brought with it significant changes in all areas of life, including tertiary education.

Tertiary education remains at the center of economic well-being, and its import may have grown due to its importance in a knowledge economy. Education is necessary for growth both through its direct contribution to skills and workforce quality and also because of the ways in which it adds key competencies such as critical thinking, creativity, teamwork and self-learning [9]. These contribute to entrepreneurship, mobility, and the capacity to process information and new ideas.

Governments and institutions need to act quickly since they exist in a competitive environment where all countries and universities interested in staying competitive are also changing [10]. In particular, regional cooperation can add value by reaching a deeper understanding of the forces for change, sharing experiences to build confidence in the ability to adjust and to capture the benefits on offer, and removing impediments to integration. The implication for higher education is that relationships among universities across regions needs to be increased and strengthened [11].

Globalization is a highly complex process that has impacted multiple national and international arenas. At times, when individuals have spoken about globalization, the term has been employed as a synonym for American imperialism as if the term simply refers to the extension throughout the world of American power and culture [12]. Although the rationale for such an assertion is understandable, such an assumption makes it appear that the USA is not influenced by globalization, as if the country is simply on a unidirectional trajectory and globalization is the next logical stage in the country's development. But globalization has impacted American universities just as well. What we need to do, then, is not work from a western perspective about what globalization is or how an institution should respond. Rather, although the forces of globalization may be similar across geographic borders, how a university will respond will largely result from national imperatives and the culture of an institution [13].

Regardless of the challenges that globalization may have created for the world's economies, and indirectly universities, one point is certain: organizations no longer can look entirely inwardly and focus on a local market as if larger forces are not at work [14]. Jobs are outsourced from one country to another. A product that a company made for decades that served a niche market suddenly finds competition from a company that is thousands of miles away. A worker spends his entire lifetime in one job, and then discovers that she is unemployed because of changes in the workplace. And universities find that they cannot rely on revenue streams that once seemed certain. Government subsidies shrink because of a new definition of public goods and educational resources. Clienteles shift because on-line learning enables students to take classes virtually, rather than having to attend class on a campus. Faculty discovers that either the compensation for a traditional academic job no longer provides a salary that enables a comfortable living, or that there are opportunities beyond academic work.

Globalization, however, does not necessarily need to portend that all of the consequences are negative for individuals or organizations. However, as I discuss below, rather than assume that stasis is the norm, the "new normal" that globalization assumes is that change must be a central component of any organization [15]. Educational organizations not only have to incorporate the notion of change into their organizational ethos, they also have to train students on how to adapt to change rather than assuming that a college education provides job security for life.

Global partnerships are an obvious outgrowth of globalization. International arrangements once meant that a university might send some students for a semester abroad. Although undergraduate travel is certainly a mainstay of academic institutions, global partnerships today involve a great deal more activities from not only students, but also faculty, and different units within a university [16]. Indeed, as I suggested above, based on an organization's culture, the environment has shifted for successful organizations that enable and encourage the actors to create global partnerships that will increase the well-being of the university.

Education is a useful example of the breadth of globalization insofar as education's reach transcends one or another category: education not only is transformed by globalization, but as knowledge-producing organizations, schools, colleges, and universities also transform globalization. Discussions often center around globalization's impact on economics, trade, or culture. Education cuts across virtually all of these categories. The result is that education, in general, and higher education, in particular, is undergoing as significant of a change as at any time in the last century, in large part because globalization assumes a knowledge-based economy [17].

The result is that the definition of a country's economy now exceeds simple geographic boundaries. Communication and transportation technologies enable companies to transcend borders in ways unimaginable only a generation ago. The same may be said of tertiary education. Where one takes classes and how one takes them and who teaches these classes—indeed, even what we mean by a "class"—is being unalterably changed in a remarkably quick timeframe.

I have previously written about how the first wave of globalization was simply the movement of students across borders [18]. The number of students in the Asia-Pacific, for example, moving overseas for their university education almost doubled between 1999 and 2006, and has continued apace. There is no reason to think these increases will not continue. The new wave of globalization, however, includes not merely teachers on the move but also programs, degrees, and institutions. And "movement" is not simply geographic travel but also participation enabled by improvements in technology and communication. The underlying ethos is one of the competitions; the World Trade Organization has estimated that the global market for education is well over US $40 billion dollars. According to a report published by the United Nations Educational, Scientific, and Cultural Organization (UNESCO), there were approximately 207 million students in tertiary education in 2014—a number that has more than doubled since 2000 and continues to increase [19].

The new wave of globalization includes the movement of teachers and whole institutions into overseas markets, joint degree programs offered by institutions in different economies, and distance learning programs, to mention just a few of its characteristics [20]. It has a higher level of commercial motivation: There is not only a shift from student mobility to program and provider mobility, but also a shift in orientation in the relationships between universities from a focus on development and cooperation to what might be defined as competitive commerce. The new wave offers access to skills in delivery, experience in curriculum design, teaching resources, quality assurance systems, and research capacity

and an international perspective, all of which can add value for local partners [21]. But it also brings competition and pressure for adjustment. The result is that our universities have to build an innovative culture.

4 Defining Innovation for Global Partnerships

Organizations change for a variety of reasons. New organizations have fewer rules. As organizations age and expand, they gain a history and a way to conduct business. Leaders have different priorities and set the organization in a new direction. Environmental conditions force an organization to react in one way or another.

Stable organizations also are different from innovative organizations. Fast food chains are not particularly innovative. When a customer enters McDonald's, he or she is not looking for an innovative hamburger. Indeed, in large part, the organization has been successful for its stability and its ability to replicate a similar experience across different countries. At the same time, local customs are observed. Similarly, the army is not looking for creative soldiers. The organization succeeds, in part, because the employees follow orders.

Thus, colleges and universities that are going to be innovative are different from organizations that require stability. One of the curiosities of academic organizations is that they frequently have creative individuals, even though the organization may not be innovative. Creativity pertains to inventiveness grounded in field-specific knowledge and expedited by motivation [22]. Indeed, successful academic organizations have fostered individual creativity through the assumption that a walled fortress divorced from the daily troubles and turmoil of society will enable a creative environment. How many poets or creative writers have used the university as a sinecure? Nobel Prize winners are overwhelmingly located at universities where tenure has provided them the time to be creative. Such organizational environments are entirely different from a prison or fast food franchise where no one wants workers to be creative.

Innovation requires a different organizational structure. Innovation pertains to the implementation of a creative product or process and its perceived novelty once it has been evaluated by a critical audience [23]. But how does an organization change its processes so it is seen as innovative? What might an innovative organization look like that is different from traditional organizations?

Prior to creating a culture of innovation, an understanding of the impediments that exist in organizations is prudent [24]. Consider traditional organizations and how they function. Regulations and standardization are the norm. Rules explain the dos and don'ts of organizational life.

Individuals learn what acceptable behavior is and how to act. Process is important. When one arrives and leaves, how someone dresses, when days may be taken for holidays, and the like are all part of clarifying acceptable behavior. In doing so, an objective is that the processes involved in enabling the organization to function are standardized so that differences do not occur. Starbucks prides itself that the taste of its café latte will be the same whether one buys it in New York, Singapore, or Dubai. Even relatively new organizations, such as Amazon, have rules and regulations that govern behavior and standardize action.

A traditional organization incentivizes activities that produce stability, rather than disruption [25]. Employees get awards for showing up on time or by having a workplace that exemplifies company codes of conduct. Thinking "out of the box" is not typically rewarded. Indeed, managers oversee actions in order to ensure that productivity is maintained at a level that the organization has stipulated. New entrants to an organization learn quickly that reporting requirements assume standardized behavior.

Even universities that reward creative behavior have rules and regulations [26]. Research and scholarship may be creative, but the organization's processes clarify the parameters within which one acts. The vision of the university as a monastery where academics were to be divorced from the daily concerns of society has enabled a rhythm and pace that framed acceptable modes of behavior. The desire to innovate —to scale up one's ideas, or to have the organization function differently from its peers—was eschewed, or at least was never a priority. Until recently, when one looked at the world's great universities, "entrepreneurial" was not a word that came to mind; indeed, an "entrepreneurial university" was not intended as a complement, for the institution in question was presumably conducting business in a manner different from what had been established.

An innovative organization rewards experimentation. Rather than being divorced from society, an innovative university is more likely to think about ways to engage with the larger environment. Such an observation is particularly important with regard to global partnerships. Bringing ideas to market is no longer disdained, but applauded. The implication is that an institution is likely to have services that augment faculty ideas in non-traditional ways rather than standardized ones. Faculty once wrote for one another via scholarly journals. Innovative organizations utilize social media so that professors are able to extend their ideas not only to their confreres but also to the larger society.

Rather than standardizing processes, innovative organizations set stable goals about what they want individuals to do and to produce; they then enable individuals to create the means of production. Rather than acceptable norms of behavior with regard to how one dresses or when one comes and goes from work, an innovative organization is more likely to focus less on micromanagement and pay more attention to goals. Autonomy within an innovative organization suggests that individuals should be encouraged to create patterns of behavior that will empower them to do their work, rather than assuming that the organization is the best determiner of organizational behavior. Difference, rather than similarity, is celebrated.

How an organization spends its time and resources is a useful clue for understanding if innovation is an organizational priority and whether global partnerships are a central part of the culture, or peripheral. Offices devised to regulate behavior may succeed in a traditional organization, but not in an innovative one. Instead, temporal and fiscal resources will be geared toward encouraging experimentation and risk. "Venture capital" is an idea outside of traditional organizations where resources are put toward experiments. By definition, an experiment may fail. An innovative organization will have internal funding mechanisms that support experimentation; in effect, the organization has an internalized form of venture capital that rewards risk [27].

Curiously, tenure was once seen as a structure that facilitated experimentation; over time, however, the concept has been turned on its head. Assistant professors commonly profess to undertaking activities that are less risky in order to publish articles that will enable them to achieve tenure. The socialization process creates a culture that gravitates against experimentation and toward conservative behavior. For the twenty-first century, academics need to revitalize structures and processes so that they reward, rather than penalize, experimentation.

Similarly, the vision of the isolated academic working on research isolated from one's colleagues and peers has to be reconsidered in an innovative environment. Rather than standardized, isolated behavior, the organization seeks distributed problem-solving. Teamwork matters. Innovative organizations encourage multiple perspectives and ideas. Rather than a solo composition, think of the metaphor of an orchestra where different players have different parts to play in order to create a brilliant piece of music. Innovative organizations encourage individual experimentation, but they also frame individual action across actors so that the outcome is unique, rather than similar.

The need for innovation is only likely to increase. Newspapers were once a mainstay of society. Only a generation ago, no one would have predicted their demise. Individuals thought of social media as entirely different from the newspaper and as something used largely by younger people. And yet, countless newspapers have been downsized or closed over the last twenty years. The ability to adapt to new environments is a skill that needs to be fostered. Hence, the assumption that higher education does not need to be innovative in a manner fundamentally different from the past is perilous. Universities need innovation to manage a potentially turbulent future—or more urgently—to avoid irrelevance.

One outgrowth of globalization and the ability of universities to incorporate innovation into their culture are seen by a growing interest in international research cooperation. The research community is being asked to respond to issues that apply across borders such as climate change, for example. Cooperation is valuable as institutions respond to these sorts of issues. Cooperation and cross-border projects have a number of advantages [28]. They include:

- building research capacity and drawing together required research expertise
- studying problems in situ
- providing research students with an international experience
- combining research beneficiaries and helping avoid problems of free-riding and therefore underfunding
- helping to capture economies of scale
- avoiding costly duplication
- capturing the benefits arising from differences in relative costs in research inputs
- gathering insights from comparative studies
- adding to the impact of research results
- reducing technology transfer costs.

My point here is that there are real drivers for international cooperation and global partnerships, far beyond mere reputation setting for newcomer or mid-ranked institutions. A generation ago, only a handful of universities might have looked across geographic borders to establish relationships, but today such activities are increasingly common. These activities are also a great deal more than simply sending students abroad or welcoming students to the host institution primarily to generate a revenue stream. Instead, a broad array of activities is being contemplated largely because globalization has both enabled and required universities to think and act in ways different from the past. What enables universities to act decisively by forging and sustaining global partnerships? I answer this question in the next section.

5 Sustaining an Innovative Environment and Building Stable Global Partnerships

I have argued that globalization requires innovation in universities that historically have traditional cultures framed by a socializing process that inculcates a mission that usually is historicist rather than forward-thinking. The organization's environment is generally local, and the information provided meets the needs of a traditional organization. Strategic plans generally seek to improve incrementally based on a traditional organizational structure. What we need to confront, however, is a new intellectual framework oriented toward change and innovation.

The challenges that academe faces to develop and sustain global partnerships in a competitive environment are numerous. Academic staff, for example, require skills different from those who taught subject matter in a classroom and conducted discrete research. Of consequence, teaching will undergo a sea-change and research will require skills associated with teamwork and cross-cultural collaboration. The result is that the kind of individuals we hire is likely to require a different framework from the past, and our universities will need pedagogical and research training centers aimed at equipping staff with skills required for a globalized universe.

As I noted above, "venture capital" is a normal term in the business world, but foreign to those of us in academic institutions. Academics generally conduct discrete research or find funding from a government agency. Global partnerships may well need venture capital from a funding arm of the university or from the business world. For such funding to occur, the skills researchers need not supplant what world-class researchers currently have, but rather necessitate additional skills of the researcher or within the university. Simply stated, a chemistry professor needs a laboratory to undertake research. In a global environment where universities hope to attract venture capital, in addition to traditional academic materials such as laboratories, universities also require technology transfer offices, units that are able to develop business plans, and offices that establish relationships with business and industry that look to marketing ideas in the natural and social sciences [29].

There is also not one predetermined manner in which universities must move. In the past, a university might have simply figured out which areas of the world they wished to send their students and created arrangements with a few institutions together with faculty exchanges. The current options are more complex. Universities need to choose a model of internationalization [30]. Program and provider mobility comes into play. An array of choices exists that decision-makers actively need to consider and accept or reject. "Brick and mortar" campuses in another country remain an option, but virtual campuses are also a possibility. Dual enrollment options exist such that one campus might offer a discrete number of courses and another institution across the world will offer the other. Some universities will see dual degrees as beneficial to their students and others might think it decreases the brand. The result is that quality assurance is no longer a "one size fits all" model but must be adapted to the mission that the institution has chosen for itself.

One conundrum of globalization is that over the last generation there has been a mania about international rankings [31]. Ministries want their institutions to be represented on league tables. The risk, of course, is that all universities then need to adhere to the same sorts of activities. Precisely at a time when a university's culture ought to choose an identity that sets itself apart from other universities, there is a pressure to conform. Over time, however, rather than a move toward isomorphism, universities are likely to establish unique global partnerships that enable innovative relationships to occur based on the unique cultures of the institutions. Organizational cultures gravitate against isomorphism as if one institution's identity is akin to another. Rather, a university needs to come to grips with its own identity, make its uniqueness clear to internal and external audiences, and then develop relationships with global partners based on those differing identities.

Markets respond to diversity and unique ideas. Not all partnerships will succeed, but the successful organization is one that is open to experimentation and trial and error. To be sure, support structures need to be in place that enable such relationships to germinate, but the future lies less in mimicking what other institutions have done and instead in building an identity based on innovation.

Because of increased collaboration across borders and a focus on differentiation rather than similarity, the import of quality assurance is likely to rise. The most obvious example is that of for-profit higher education in the USA. New providers entered the academic market and their experimentation gained initial admiration. Over time, the experiments were cause for concern. Low completion rates, increased costs, and fraudulent claims plagued the industry when governmental and accrediting agencies investigated its activities [32]. The same sort of oversight needs to be done with the ventures universities begin across the globe to ensure that the activity is of high quality and measurable cost. An increase in global partnerships suggests that a Ministry of Higher Education's role is likely to move from a funding agent to that of a design or certification authority. The likelihood also exists that cross-border collaboration will require cross-border alignments of those who determine quality assurance.

Universities interested in building global partnerships obviously need offices focused on the matter, but to build a regional and global community, a variety of mutual topics need to be discussed. Commonsensically, global partnerships require multiple partners. A first step is to develop new data collection systems that will be utilized by those groups who are working together. Institutions can be proprietary about their university's data, and global partnerships require the opposite sort of action. Data sharing, especially among institutions without a history of data collection and analysis is an initial step for successful collaboration.

The sharing of data, however, is simply a first step in regional cooperation that needs to be considered, developed, and enhanced over time. Universities in developing economies often face a severe "brain drain" that needs to be reversed [33]. Global partnerships in open markets suggest not simply an economic free trade zone, but also an academic one where faculty participates actively at more than their home institution.

Similarly, rather than a reliance on national professional and disciplinary associations that cater to a local clientele, cross-border associations can work together to increase the teaching and research capacity of the academic staff in the region. Just as global partnerships suggest increased student and academic mobility, so too might staff mobility be enhanced. The key component here is a commitment to openness, experimentation, and rigor in the mode of supply.

Research cooperation also will be reconfigured. Rather than research project "A" being done in one institution and research project "B" in another, there ought to be a proliferation in modes of supply. The joint funding of Ph.D. programs, for example, is one possibility for partnerships where faculty and students from multiple institutions work together on projects that are of regional benefit and enable students to gain skills aimed at the future rather than the past. Students trained on more than one campus return to their host university with networks and skills not ordinarily gained in a discrete program.

Although I have argued here for a changed organizational culture aimed at innovation in an era of globalization, of necessity, one key player in the environment needs to be addressed. Universities are located in countries and in one manner or another they are framed by the stance a country takes toward its neighbors and toward education. A country can enhance or restrict global partnerships based on its willingness to have its institution engage in such activities. As opposed to previous opportunities, however, a country does not necessarily need to provide long-standing revenue for an activity. Nevertheless, a country also has to be willing to enable its institutions to operate in ways that may be at odds with the cultural or economic mores of the country. "Venture capital," for example, is not a phrase commonly used in socialist countries, but I have suggested such an arrangement might be beneficial for a university seeking a global partnership.

How faculty thinks and works is not only framed by an academic culture but also by the national culture from which they come. In general, I see such differences as a strength, and institutions and faculties can work out their differences, but if a nation state is wary of such collaborations, then long-standing partnerships are going to be at risk. An initial step is for a ministry and its institutions to develop codes of conduct that enable the ground rules to be understood. Finely tuned, restrictive rules are less likely to enable collaboration then models aimed at enabling partnerships. Any country has a vested interest in seeing its universities prosper, but in general, steering global partnerships from afar, such as from the ministry, is less likely to produce sustainable projects. Those closest to the project are the best qualified to determine the parameters of the project.

6 Conclusion

I have approached global partnerships as entering a new era because of globalization. Although universities always have had unique cultures, I have suggested that rather than aiming at maintaining the status quo, the culture now needs to shift toward innovation. Such movements certainly come with risks, but also rewards. A successful university aimed at innovation and increasing global partnerships will acknowledge that not all such ventures will succeed. Nevertheless, the parameters of what is necessary for global partnerships will be apparent. Such projects do not simply occur without cultural and structural supports both within the university and at the Ministry level.

The future holds great possibility for new sorts of arrangements that go far beyond simply shipping students to one or another country or for singular faculty exchanges. The potential for arrangements that work at resolving some of the world's more intransigent social and environmental ills are significant. The question is if our institutions have the ability to reorient themselves toward long-standing arrangements that enable our students, faculty and staff to function and prosper in new ways.

References

1. Brody, W. (2007). College goes global. *Foreign Affairs, 86*(20), 122–133.
2. Knight, G. A., & Cavusgil, S. T. (2004). Innovation, organizational capabilities, and the born-global firm. *Journal of International Business Studies, 35*(2), 124–141.
3. Stensaker, B. (2018). Academic development as cultural work: Responding to the organizational complexity of modern higher education institutions. *International Journal for Academic Development, 23*(4), 274–285.
4. Tierney, W. G., & Lanford, M. (2018). Research in higher education: Cultural perspectives. In J. C. Shin & P. N. Teixeira (Eds.), *Encyclopedia of international higher education systems and institutions* (pp. 1–6). Dordrecht: Springer.
5. Chaffee, E. E., & Tierney, W. G. (1988). *Collegiate culture and leadership strategies.* New York: MacMillan.
6. Tierney, W. G. (2008). *The impact of culture on organizational decision making.* Sterling, VA: Stylus.
7. Tierney, W. G., & Lanford, M. (2018). Institutional culture in higher education. In J. C. Shin & P. N. Teixeira (Eds.), *Encyclopedia of international higher education systems and institutions* (pp. 1–7). Dordrecht: Springer.
8. Gilpin, R. (2000). *The challenge of global capitalism: The world economy in the 21st century.* Princeton, NJ: Princeton University Press.
9. Lanford, M. (2016). Perceptions of higher education reform in Hong Kong: A glocalization perspective. *International Journal of Comparative Education and Development, 18*(3), 184–204.
10. Douglass, J. (2009). *Higher education's new global order: How and why governments are creating structured opportunity markets.* Berkeley, CA: Center for Studies in Higher Education.
11. Altbach, P. G., & Knight, J. (2007). The internationalization of higher education: Motivations and realities. *Journal of Studies in International Education, 11*(3–4), 290–305.
12. Held, D., & McGrew, A. (2007). *Globalization theory: Approaches and controversies.* Cambridge: Polity Press.
13. Salmi, J. (2011). The road to academic excellence: Lessons of experience. In P. G. Altbach & J. Salmi (Eds.), *The road to academic excellence: The making of world-class research universities* (pp. 323–347). Washington, DC: World Bank.
14. Marginson, S. (2004). Competition and markets in higher education: A "glonacal" analysis. *Policy Futures in Education, 2*(2), 175–244.
15. Salmi, J. (2002). New challenges for tertiary education: The World Bank report. *International Higher Education, 28,* 7–9.
16. Lanford, M., & Tierney, W. G. (2016). The international branch campus: Cloistered community or agent of social change? In D. Neubauer, J. Hawkins, M. Lee, & C. Collins (Eds.), *The Palgrave handbook of Asia Pacific higher education* (pp. 157–172). New York: Palgrave Macmillan.
17. Florida, R. (2014). The creative class and economic development. *Economic Development Quarterly, 28*(3), 196–205.
18. Tierney, W. G. (2010). Introduction and overview. In C. Findlay & W. G. Tierney (Eds.), *Globalisation and tertiary education in the Asia-Pacific: The changing nature of a dynamic market* (pp. 1–16). Toh Tuck, Singapore: World Scientific.
19. United Nations Educational, Scientific, and Cultural Organization (UNESCO). (2017). *Six ways to ensure higher education leaves no one behind.* Paris: UNESCO.
20. Tierney, W. G., & Lanford, M. (2015). An investigation of the impact of international branch campuses on organizational culture. *Higher Education, 70*(2), 283–298.
21. Knight, J. (2010). Cross-border higher education: Quality assurance and accreditation issues and implications. In C. Findlay & W. G. Tierney (Eds.), *Globalisation and tertiary education in the Asia-Pacific: The changing nature of a dynamic market* (pp. 73–92). Toh Tuck, Singapore: World Scientific.
22. Tierney, W. G., & Lanford, M. (2016). Conceptualizing innovation in higher education. In M. B. Paulsen (Ed.), *Higher education: Handbook of theory and research* (Vol. 31, pp. 1–40). Dordrecht: Springer.
23. Tierney, W. G., & Lanford, M. (2016). *Cultivating strategic innovation in higher education.* New York: TIAA-CREF Institute.
24. Brewer, D. C., & Tierney, W. G. (2011). Barriers to innovation in U.S. higher education. In B. Wildavsky, A. P. Kelly, & K. Carey (Eds.), *Reinventing higher education: The promise of innovation* (pp. 11–40). Cambridge, MA: Harvard Education Press.
25. Christensen, C. M., & Eyring, H. J. (2011). *The innovative university: Changing the DNA of higher education from the inside out.* San Francisco, CA: Jossey-Bass.
26. Tierney, W. G. (2012). Creativity and organizational culture. In M. N. Bastedo (Ed.), *The organization of higher education: Managing colleges for a new era* (pp. 160–180). Baltimore, MD: Johns Hopkins University Press.

27. Drucker, P. F. (2014). *Innovation and entrepreneurship*. New York: Routledge.
28. Knight, J. (2011). Education hubs: A fad, a brand, an innovation? *Journal of Studies in International Education, 15*(3), 221–240.
29. Slaughter, S., & Rhoades, G. (2004). *Academic capitalism and the new economy: Markets, state, and higher education*. Baltimore, MD: Johns Hopkins University Press.
30. Knight, J. (2015). International universities: Misunderstandings and emerging models? *Journal of Studies in International Education, 19*(2), 107–121.
31. Tierney, W. G., & Lanford, M. (2017). Between massification and globalization: Is there a role for global university rankings? In E. Hazelkorn (Ed.), *Global rankings and the geopolitics of higher education* (pp. 295–308). Oxford: Routledge.
32. Angula, A. J. (2016). *Diploma mills*. Baltimore, MD: Johns Hopkins University Press.
33. Docquier, F., Lohest, O., & Marfouk, A. (2007). Brain drain in developing countries. *World Bank Economic Review, 21*(2), 193–218.

Open Access This chapter is licensed under the terms of the Creative Commons Attribution 4.0 International License (http://creativecommons.org/licenses/by/4.0/), which permits use, sharing, adaptation, distribution and reproduction in any medium or format, as long as you give appropriate credit to the original author(s) and the source, provide a link to the Creative Commons license and indicate if changes were made.

The images or other third party material in this chapter are included in the chapter's Creative Commons license, unless indicated otherwise in a credit line to the material. If material is not included in the chapter's Creative Commons license and your intended use is not permitted by statutory regulation or exceeds the permitted use, you will need to obtain permission directly from the copyright holder.

Global Citizens for the Twenty-First Century: The Role of International Partnerships in University Education

Feridun Hamdullahpur

1 Introduction

The scale of disruption that our world faces from geopolitical to socioeconomic perspectives is vast. No single researcher, university or nation can achieve a breakthrough solution alone. The challenges are too complex, and finding success is only possible when we work together as a global community of educators, researchers and influencers.

At the heart of this is the need to collaborate across borders, languages, industries and disciplines. The challenges and opportunities in our disruptive world are only becoming more complex due to the acceleration of new technology, an ageing population in the West, an increasingly turbulent geopolitical landscape and more.

This chapter will explore the role international partnerships have for universities and how they educate, research and impact a disruptive future.

Cross-discipline cooperation has long been the focus of many institutions to increase the impact of research and the strength of our students' education. This approach can also be taken through international partnerships that leverage the combined power of talent, resources and vision that spans national boundaries and cultures. Our increasingly globalized world offers a range of opportunities for university education to grow and flourish at the individual level, institutional level and the national and global levels.

It is vital that international partnerships also bring together a range of partners that intersect with all aspects of our society. This means broadening the scope of traditional partnerships between universities to include partners in government, industry and Non-Governmental Organizations (NGOs).

And, how we develop international work-integrated learning opportunities will make the difference in our ability as universities to develop global talent when we need their leadership the most.

2 Achieving the Three Levels of Collaboration Success

Internationalization within post-secondary institutions has evolved into a mosaic of programs and partnerships that look nothing like those seen in past decades [1]. Each international partnership is unique and has developed to suit a specific need for the institution, researchers or students involved.

A university's expertise, scope and goals are individual to their community of students, faculty and community members. While each collaboration has individual characteristics that make it ideal for both or multiple parties involved, achieving wide-ranging success in international partnerships means developing partnerships that have an Individual Impact, Institutional Impact and a National and Global Impact.

Implementing actionable programs that touch on each of these levels is vital in creating lasting and comprehensive international partnerships for universities. Because of the central role universities play in educating the world's citizens and their leadership in scientific, technological and policy research, achieving success at each level is the ideal approach for broad impact.

2.1 Individual Impact

The Individual Impact of international partnerships most often comes in the form of student exchanges. The intrinsic characteristic of universities viewing the free flow of ideas that transcend borders, conflict and cultures as being very valuable has made international exchanges standard practice at most institutions around the world. As our world has become smaller and more globalized, the value of international experiences for students has only increased.

F. Hamdullahpur (✉)
University of Waterloo, Waterloo, Canada
e-mail: president@uwaterloo.ca

© The Author(s) 2020
A. Al-Youbi et al. (eds.), *Successful Global Collaborations in Higher Education Institutions*,
https://doi.org/10.1007/978-3-030-25525-1_3

Increasing the ability of students to gain a global perspective through short-term and long-term exchanges offers valuable experiences for students that transcend their learning in the classroom. Offering and hosting exchange students from partnering institutions from around the world creates a lasting impact on the students involved that is immediately felt upon the completion of their education.

A survey of Asian companies found that 57% of surveyed companies agreed that hiring international talent is very important or somewhat important [2]. The demand is there for the talent, and students understand that there is significant value in international exchanges that can increase their career prospects.

The Erasmus Impact Study [3], which surveys European Union students in exchange programs, found in 2013 that the rate of unemployment for students who had studied abroad was 23% lower than those who had remained in their home country. This is not insignificant in the minds of students who are looking to their future prospects for employment throughout their university career.

Developing exchange offerings for students ultimately depends on establishing positive relationships with partner institutions with similar academic and research programs. Creating a framework that is mutually beneficial for both institutions and students create a good foundation for long-term relationships. To make these relationships and experiences as positive as possible, each university must ensure a cohesive process of bringing international students into their campus community.

There are also typical barriers international students face that need to be addressed to ensure a successful student exchange for all parties involved. These considerations include most pressingly, financial limitations that limit the ability for students to explore the world. Considerations also include screening for positive academic prerequisites, so students have the educational background needed to succeed, language support for those students arriving in a country that is not their native tongue, community integration services that bring exchange students into the greater university community, and the student mental health and wellness supports needed to serve international exchange students.

Many of these elements and expectations should be well-defined in the student exchange agreement to ensure that the responsibilities of each institution are clear to each party. Institutions can begin the exploration of such exchanges through a preliminary memorandum of understanding (MoU), but a formal agreement that is signed between both parties is necessary in the end.

Given different national and institutional cultures are at play when developing these agreements, what is customary at one institution or in one country may not be at another. Establishing expectations for each party ahead of time will help mitigate disagreements and possible legal issues that may arise in the future.

Embracing exchange students and the potential they have to add to the diversity of ideas and perspectives will strengthen the hosting university as the blending of cultures and experiences spreads throughout the domestic student population. The links that are created across nations and institutions start at the individual level and can last lifetimes. The impact is significant on the individual student involved, but also lends to what is possible at the institutional level when international partnerships are established.

2.2 Institutional Impact

The second level of international collaboration that is integral to developing successful partnerships is those that have an Institutional Impact. Institutional Impact collaborations are primarily found at the research level. This includes, but is not limited to, joint research projects, co-authoring of research papers and the sharing of resources through joint research grants and research equipment use.

With the ever-present challenge of raising funds and the resources needed for any number of research projects, it can be difficult for any institution to have the equipment and field expertise to meet the curiosity and vision of their researchers. To meet this demand, like-minded universities from around the world can find common ground and partner on projects and work together towards discovery.

This can be joint research projects between disciplines to maximize institutional expertise or formally pooling resources to fund large-scale joint projects on previously agreed upon areas of focus. By building complementary agreements that lean into the strengths of each institution, there are more opportunities to make an impact across disciplines and fields. This can bolster the output from each institution that would not have been possible prior to the agreements.

Assessing the success of these programs can be established through several performance indicators that are individual to each project and institution. Traditional indicators include the number of joint research papers that are authored between the partnering institutions and the number of joint research grants awarded through the added strength of the collaboration.

Further to the partnerships between institutions is the addition of collaborations between universities and industry partners. The development of international research agreements between universities and businesses that are not domestically connected is becoming a commonplace. The transfer of ideas and innovations through collaborative R&D between academia and industry lends to an impact at the institutional level that creates generally positive outcomes for everyone involved.

According to a study in *The Journal of Technology and Transfer*, industry partners enjoy the benefit of having access to groundbreaking research and talent pools, and universities find a source of revenue to fund graduate student work and often the addition of needed equipment. This makes both parties likely to expand on more project collaborations in the future [4].

It was pointed out in the Individual Impact section the impact student mobility and exchanges can have on those students taking part in a cross-cultural experience. A similar benefit can be found at the Institutional Impact level through staff exchanges. Staff exchanges between institutions and cultures can have a fundamental impact on the innovative ability of any university through the exploration of how their peers from around the world face common challenges in their work.

These exchanges can include a university's communications team travelling to a partnering institution to collaborate and explore joint projects or a staff member travelling to another university to speak with and/or shadow a peer of theirs to experience their culture and share industry best practices. Universities hold a tremendous amount of talent in their staff and the power of collaboration amongst this community group can be leveraged both for closer relationships between individuals and to make improvements at an institutional level.

Universities have an opportunity to add to their research capabilities through collaborations that aim to bring like-minded institutions and researchers together. The impact of these collaborations can be highly valuable. In addition, through partnerships with the private sector and embracing an entrepreneurial spirit of discovery and creation, universities can be impactful on a whole other level that has significant implications nationally and globally.

2.3 National and Global Impact

Remaining at this level of international cooperation can be both fruitful and limiting at the same time. Individual and Institutional Impact keep the emphasis of positive collaborations within the realm of student and university. While these programs can create strong impacts on the personal and institutional level, there is further room to grow international collaborations so they can have national and global impacts.

International programs that promote entrepreneurial enterprises and the development of university intellectual property into commercialized ventures will have the ability to shape and impact society at a far greater scale than institutional and individual levels. For many institutions, this can be a challenge to implement as it is counter to their established practices and can face resistance at a faculty level.

A number of universities around the world are making entrepreneurship a priority for their students, but what is often lost is the importance of international collaborations in developing technology and intellectual property (IP) that can have a global impact.

Growth within regional and global economies can be produced through a university's dedication to supporting entrepreneurship and innovative IP policy for students and researchers [5]. Coordinating with international partners through joint ventures and research projects with an eye on the commercialization of research makes the impact far greater than the act of discovery. Bringing innovations to the world and understanding global markets through international partnerships bring an element of coordination and global experience that students, faculty and alumni can use to their advantage down the road.

Creating international entrepreneurial experiences for students and faculty is a key in having a national and global impact that creates economic prosperity and provides a primer for future technological and scientific discoveries.

Challenges to the establishment of global ventures rest at the institutional and legal limitations of each partnering organization. Each university must adhere to a form of creator-owned IP policy that removes the barrier of who owns the IP by keeping the ownership with the researchers involved and not the university. This will fuel the desire and opportunity for more researcher-driven ventures as it incentivizes commercialization and limits any legal issues that may come to pass between partnering institutions.

It is equally as important that the partnering organizations promote entrepreneurship at their universities at a fundamental level. A creator-friendly IP policy is vital towards promoting entrepreneurship but additional supports such as mentoring, commercialization expertise and basic startup programs for researchers are integral to future success. Adding international experiences through research partnerships and international work-integrated learning experiences for students, such as cooperative education job placements, contributes to the future impact of international partnerships.

It is understandable that every university within their national border would want to contribute and be a part of building a strong, healthy economy through talent, knowledge and, more so, the integration of the two in the simplest form of entrepreneurship. However, many large-scale challenges (i.e. water scarcity, climate change, artificial intelligence) are of a global scale, and we need to understand and accept the importance and value of sharing and building solutions together with other nations through collaborations.

Of the nearly 200 million students who are enroled in universities and colleges worldwide, about 5 million of them study at institutions outside of their home countries [6]. This provides a tremendous amount of mobility of knowledge, culture, global awareness and opportunity.

And, since the world is in great need of collective learning from one another and building healthy economies worldwide, what could be a better opportunity to collaborate globally to achieve prosperity for all?

3 The Wide Range of University Partnerships

Knowing that there is a range of international collaborations possible for a university broadens its ability to find the perfect institutional fit whether it is with another university, private enterprise, government or NGO. Partnerships are not limited to what can be traditionally thought of as academic exchanges of students and ideas, but can also be viewed as an act of collaboration that creates something neither organization could achieve on its own impact.

It is vital to weave collaborations together and build a network of cooperation that is complementary to all parties. Given the central role of universities to be centres of excellence where society comes to educate the next generation and find the discoveries that will drive future prosperity, ensuring all avenues of international cooperation are leveraged will strengthen outcomes and contribute a level of diversification needed in our complex, globalized economy [7].

There are several examples of these varying partnerships that can be found at the University of Waterloo.

3.1 Soochow University, University of Waterloo and Suzhou Industrial Park Joint Institute of Research and Education on Nanotechnology

International partnerships can be tailored for comprehensive impact. While these partnerships add new layers of complexity to both build and sustain, they also have the opportunity to create positive outcomes that cross borders even outside of academia.

The strong and productive research partnership between the University of Waterloo's Waterloo Institute for Nanotechnology (WIN) and the Soochow University started in 2011 when Soochow University, the University of Waterloo and the Suzhou Industrial Park (SUN-WIN-SIP) initiated a Joint Institute of Research and Education. The objectives of the Joint Institute are to enable faculty at both institutions to engage in research collaborations, foster scholar exchange and stimulate entrepreneurship and innovation in nanotechnology [8].

The partnership is made up of several programs and agreements that blend research, education and commercialization that are aided by SIP and Waterloo's spirit of entrepreneurship and creator-friendly IP policy.

The research collaboration has shown to be productive as SUN and SIP have sponsored 24 collaborative SUN-WIN research projects in each of the four key theme areas of nanotechnology, namely nanoinstrumentation, nanobiosystems, nanoelectronics and nanomaterials development, since April 2012.

The first round of funding sponsored 12 projects, ten of which received 450,000 RMB (approximately $70,000 CAD) and two of which received 750,000 RMB (approximately $150,000 CAD) over three years. In 2013, seven additional projects were awarded 450,000 RMB each, and in 2015 five projects received the same.

During the initial phase of the collaboration process, Soochow University's Technology Transfer Office visited WIN in July 2012 to learn more about the University of Waterloo's commercialization practices, IP policies, entrepreneurship and faculty support. The University of Waterloo has a progressive creator-owned IP Policy that is unique amongst most universities around the world and has aided in Waterloo's researchers and students creating hundreds of startup ventures that include successful technology companies.

The partnership also brought graduate and undergraduate students into the agreement. Soochow University and WIN have signed agreements on collaborative educational programs for Soochow students interested in studying nanotechnology at the University of Waterloo, including the Doctoral program and the 3+1+1 joint Bachelor's/Master's program. In addition, WIN hosts several fourth-year Soochow students for a four-month research internship program which is sponsored by the China Scholarship Council.

This has allowed the University of Waterloo to attract top international graduate students to WIN and the university, and Soochow can offer their students the experience of studying at one of Canada's top nanotechnology labs.

Since the beginning of the nanotechnology collaboration between the University of Waterloo and Soochow, there has only been growth. These successes have also inspired the exploration of creating further agreements with additional fields of study, such as Energy and the Water Institute.

What began as an international research collaboration has flourished into a multidimensional partnership that has had fundamental Individual Impact, Institutional Impact and, with the focus on entrepreneurship, National and Global Impact.

3.2 United Nations Sustainable Development Solutions Network

As discussed in the previous sections, universities have a central role in bringing international partners from all sectors of society together to face some of the most pressing challenges facing our world. An example of this effort that can have far-reaching national and international implications can be found in the partnership the University of Waterloo established with the United Nations Sustainable Development Solutions Network (SDSN).

The SDSN is a global initiative by the United Nations dedicated to mobilizing the global community of scientific and technological talent to help promote the UN's 17 Sustainable Development Goals (SDGs) and help their nations meet their SDG targets. The majority of the work is done on the ground in regional and national SDSN hubs that can bring together those researchers, policy-makers and society members who wish to help reach their nation's SDG targets. All of this is done in an effort to accelerate an integrated approach to building a more sustainable world.

In May of 2018, the University of Waterloo became the founding institution of Canada's national SDSN hub: SDSN Canada. SDSN Canada is the country's hub of sustainability action that links hundreds of researchers and organizations that are dedicated to meeting Canada's SDG targets.

What the establishment of SDSN Canada at the University of Waterloo means for the institution is twofold. First, the University of Waterloo builds a stronger connection with a major international organization in the SDSN and also with the United Nations itself. Secondly, Waterloo becomes a national beacon, in academia, government and the rest of society, for the successful movement towards building a more sustainable world.

This increases the number of researchers, NGOs and universities from across Canada and the world which look to Waterloo as a leader in sustainability research and practices. Ten Canadian universities and NGOs have partnered with SDSN Canada in less than a year of operation [9]. These organizations are bringing their expertise and ideas to the University of Waterloo because of the institution's international partnership.

National recognition is being paid to the University of Waterloo, but it is important to note that the university is also now linked with 24 other regional and national SDSN networks from around the world. These connections are more than reputational as they can act as greater opportunities for sharing best practices and they can potentially result in future international research projects.

While the university is seeing all of this activity, SDSN Global and the United Nations have found a dedicated and capable partner to lead their Canadian SDG efforts. It is a mutually beneficial partnership that has national and global benefits for the University of Waterloo, but this partnership was not accidental.

SDSN Canada rests within the University of Waterloo's Faculty of Environment. This is the largest Faculty of Environment in Canada with the capabilities and talent of few other institutions within Canada, but the faculty also had the forethought to apply to SDSN Global to be SDSN Canada's founding institution to see what it could become.

The projects that will stem from SDSN Canada will make an impact on Canada's future prosperity, and it will do so because of this unique and successful international collaboration between universities and national and international NGOs.

3.3 Risk Management, Economic Sustainability and Actuarial Science Development in Indonesia

University partnerships can naturally take different forms with many different goals and partners. Universities can not only partner with international institutions and governments, but also be an agent of global change with the support of their national government.

An example of this type of partnership can be found in the University of Waterloo's collaboration with the Department of Global Affairs Canada (GAC), international insurance companies Manulife Indonesia and Sun Life Asia and seven Indonesian universities to create Risk Management, Economical Sustainability and Actuarial Science Development in Indonesia (READI) [10]. With funding support from the GAC, Manulife and Sun Life, the READI project aims to establish Indonesia as a regional centre of actuarial excellence.

The University of Waterloo operates as the Canadian Executing Agency for the project through the area expertise of its Department of Statistics and Actuarial Science. As the executing agency, Waterloo's role in this multilateral, international partnership is to help train and facilitate long-lasting capacity within Indonesian universities to promote and train actuaries in their home institutions.

On a broader level, this partnership endeavours to increase the number and quality of Indonesian actuarial science graduates, strengthen the linkages between industry, government and educational institutions in support of actuarial science and risk management and deepen the understanding of actuarial science and risk management as a profession in Indonesia. This effort comes at a pivotal time in the South-Asian region.

Indonesia and the entire Ring of Fire region around the Pacific Ocean face natural disasters on a regular basis, such as the devastating tsunami that hit Indonesia in 2004. These incidents bring loss of life and loss of property at significant levels. The insurance and pension industry helps provide safety nets that keep losses from being overwhelming, which allow people to rebuild their lives following disasters, and helps people to build and protect prosperity.

Without actuaries, or without enough actuaries, the ability of poor and middle-income people to access insurance, pensions and retirement plans is compromised, leaving future prosperity in the wake of disasters uncertain. That is the situation in Indonesia.

The READI partnership crosses borders and industries, brings expertise and resources from the established Department of Statistics and Actuarial Science and works with the Indonesian government and partner universities to offer joint programs. These programs include both cooperative education opportunities to build work experience and industry outreach to develop a pipeline of talent for the Indonesian economy. The global business partners are also integral when developing co-op opportunities and future job prospects for those students taking part in the READI project.

Partnerships such as this are only possible with the support of all parties. If the governments on either side were opposed to the collaboration or indifferent, it would not have the momentum to move forward. If the industry partners were not established, an essential piece of the project would be missing in the form of local and sector expertise and the loss of a recruitment partner for future actuarial talent. And, without the buy-in from the University of Waterloo or the seven partnering institutions in Indonesia, there would be no capacity to run an ongoing collaboration to promote and train the next generation of actuaries in Indonesia.

The READI project is an example of what can happen when government, industry and institutions of higher learning come together to solve a pressing problem that impacts thousands of lives when they need support the most. Every nation requires the right training and the right talent. Sharing knowledge and expertise from one institution to an international partner is at the heart of how international partnerships can make a positive impact and create long-lasting prosperity.

4 International Work-Integrated Learning: Future of Global Talent

Well-developed and well-executed international partnerships that universities take part in can fundamentally impact entire disciplines and industries. The collaboration of groundbreaking, fundamental research is only strengthened by complementary institutions working together and leveraging a global community of talented researchers.

At the heart of our institutions, despite all of the exceptional research that is done every day, our students and their growth are our top priority. Their development and future success will have an unprecedented impact on our world, but it is vital that universities leverage their global connections to offer their students a global experience that goes beyond student exchanges and joint degrees.

Work-integrated learning and experiential education have been instrumental in the development of students at the University of Waterloo through its co-op program. As pointed out in the previous section on the READI program, it is even a sought-after aspect of that international project. This is because co-op offers students a unique opportunity to gain relevant work experience throughout their degree, build a number of valuable skills outside of the classroom and earn money to pay for their studies. These experiences also cut down on the learning curve students face when leaving their institution.

Building international work-integrated learning opportunities takes this even further by introducing all of the benefits cooperative education offers and combining them with the benefits of an exchange student's experience. There is no doubt that cooperative education and student exchange programs offer distinct benefits and opportunities [11]. It is the experience at the University of Waterloo that the development of truly global talent is found at the cross section of these two programs.

Establishing these experiences does not happen overnight and depends greatly on building international partnerships with businesses overseas. Creating the linkages with businesses needed to build the network of job opportunities open to students can be done through several approaches, and they come from fostering international collaboration with their own community. Universities of all sizes have connections outside of their country in the form of other partnering institutions and their alumni.

The University of Waterloo, which was founded in 1957 has more than 15,000 alumni outside of Canada in 145 countries. These international members of the Waterloo community prove to be essential in the global expansion of co-op job opportunities, regardless of whether they are in roles that allow them to hire students for co-op positions. These alumni are advocates for a co-op at the company overseas and can act as an outpost for future placement opportunities. Moreover, the existing international partnerships the universities have with other institutions can play a significant role in developing international work-integrated learning opportunities as the students can work in research labs or on those research projects that have joint partnerships with private enterprises.

It is important to note that international experiences through experiential education should not be limited to domestic students, but to all students. There is a natural inclination to view international work placements as something domestic students seek out since international students are already taking part in an international exchange program [12]. In our experience at the University of Waterloo, this is not true.

The University of Waterloo attracts thousands of international students to our campus, not only because of our research and educational strengths but also because of our co-op program. These types of international placements happen every term and every year. One recent international co-op experience involved an international student who originally came to Waterloo from India did his co-op work term at a research lab at a partnering university in China and collaborated with one of his colleagues in China to together develop their own startup venture after completing their degrees.

This student embodies what is possible when international collaborations are combined with the power of work-integrated learning. Developing the connections, global perspective and work experience needed to inspire a transnational startup venture, by the student's own admission, could not have happened for him in India. The connections we make and the prospects that they create are only possible when we explore what is possible.

These opportunities show students that their impact can be on more than a single city or country, but on a global scale. They are opened up to a new culture and a new way of thinking that goes far beyond a classroom. The future of our world is a global one, and the right talent is needed to lead to that future. Future leaders must possess not only exceptional technical skills, but also the ability to look at problems through a global lens. Only then will we have the capability and capacity to create long-term prosperity for our world.

5 Conclusion

Partnerships offer the benefit of possibility. More ideas, resources and expertise create more opportunities for groundbreaking discoveries and the broadening of the perspectives and knowledge base of those students who take part in international experiences. These actions of institutional cooperation are integral as we look to tackle countless global challenges. Universities that limit their view of partnerships to domestic partners limit what is possible and the impact of their community of students, faculty and graduates.

Collaborations can mean many different things to many universities. To build a global network of partnerships that will lead to a prosperous twenty-first century, it would be advantageous for universities worldwide to take a holistic approach and explore the wide range of opportunities open to their institutions. There is no single area of collaboration, whether it be research, student exchange or entrepreneurship that will create the impact we need to solve the global challenges in front of us.

University education is no longer built on the learning from a handful of classrooms and instructors in an isolated campus cut-off from society. Society and the global economy are best served when our universities and their community of students, scholars and staff members branch out to develop international partners that multiply impact and opportunities to shape a more prosperous future, domestically and globally.

As certain nations in the world, out of fear, look inward instead of outward to build prosperity, our world is limited. Instead, we can set a different example for the global landscape and work together through cohesive and mutually beneficial partnerships. We are only limited by our institutions' drive and determination, and universities can and should be central to this movement. We are stronger when we work together, and with all the opportunities out there still to be seized, now is the time for universities to look across borders, cultures and disciplines to create lines of communication and collaboration.

References

1. Knight, J., & De Wit, H. (2018). Internationalization of higher education: Past and future. *International Higher Education, 95,* 2–4. https://doi.org/10.6017/ihe.2018.95.10715.
2. Walters, R. How to attract and retain the right talent to grow business internationally. https://www.robertwalters.cn/a-guide-for-asian-companies.html. Accessed March 28, 2019.
3. European Commission. (2014). Effects of mobility on the skills and employability of students and the internationalisation of higher education institutions. The Erasmus Impact Study. https://doi.org/10.2766/75468.
4. Lee, Y. S. (2000). The sustainability of university-industry research collaboration: An empirical assessment. *The Journal of Technology Transfer, 25,* 111. https://doi.org/10.1023/A:1007895322042.
5. Bramwell, A., & Wolfe, A. D. (2008). Universities and regional economic development: The entrepreneurial University of Waterloo. *Research Policy, 37*(8), 1175–1187. https://doi.org/10.1016/j.respol.2008.04.016.
6. United Nations Educational, Scientific and Cultural Organization. (2017). *Policy paper: Six ways to ensure higher education leaves no one behind* (Vol. 30). Global education monitoring report. http://unesdoc.unesco.org/images/0024/002478/247862E.pdf.
7. Banks, C., Siebe-Herbig, B., & Norton, K. (2016). *Global perspectives on strategic international partnerships: A guide to building sustainable academic linkages.* New York: Institute of International Education.
8. Waterloo Institute for Nanotechnology, International partnerships, WIN-Soochow University (SUN), Institute for Functional Nano- and Soft-Materials (FUNSOM), & The College of Nanoscience and Technology (CNST). https://uwaterloo.ca/institute-nanotechnology/partnership-and-collaboration/international/china. Accessed March 28, 2019.
9. Sustainable Development Solutions Network (SDSN) Canada, Network Members. https://uwaterloo.ca/sustainable-development-solutions-network-canada/network-members. Accessed March 28, 2019.
10. Risk Management, Economic Sustainability, and Actuarial Science Development in Indonesia. https://uwaterloo.ca/risk-management-economic-sustainability-actuarial-science-development-indonesia/. Accessed March 28, 2019.
11. McRae, N., Ramji, K., Lu, L., & Lesperance, M. (2016). Developing global-ready graduates: The CANEU-COOP experience. *Asia-Pacific Journal of Cooperative Education, 17*(4), 377–386. https://eric.ed.gov/?id=EJ1131552.

12. Gribble, C., & McRae, N. (2017). Creating a climate for global WIL: Barriers to participation and strategies for enhancing international students' involvement in WIL in Canada and Australia. In G. Barton & K. Hartwig (Eds.), *Professional learning in the work place for international students. Professional and practice-based learning* (pp. 35–55). Cham, Switzerland: Springer. https://doi.org/10.1007/978-3-319-60058-1.

Open Access This chapter is licensed under the terms of the Creative Commons Attribution 4.0 International License (http://creativecommons.org/licenses/by/4.0/), which permits use, sharing, adaptation, distribution and reproduction in any medium or format, as long as you give appropriate credit to the original author(s) and the source, provide a link to the Creative Commons license and indicate if changes were made.

The images or other third party material in this chapter are included in the chapter's Creative Commons license, unless indicated otherwise in a credit line to the material. If material is not included in the chapter's Creative Commons license and your intended use is not permitted by statutory regulation or exceeds the permitted use, you will need to obtain permission directly from the copyright holder.

International Cooperation in East Asian Higher Education

4

Gerard A. Postiglione

1 Introduction: The Rise of Asia

Asia is positioned to be the global economic hub by mid-century. It accounted for 40.9% of global gross domestic product (GDP) in 2016, an increase of 11.5% since 2000 [1–3]. Three countries—China, India, and Japan accounted for about 70% of Asia's total output in 2016. The rapidly growing population of Asia stands at 4.1 billion people or 55% of the global population. For Asia to constitute more than half of global GDP by 2050, it must raise the quality, diversity, and autonomy of its institutions of higher education [4, 5]. Therefore, Asia needs to be strategic in its international cooperation, with a shifting balance between two patterns of cooperation: traditional patterns of international cooperation with countries of the industrialized Western world and international cooperation with the rapidly emerging nations within the surrounding Asian region. Eastern Asia has become the leading edge of Asia's higher education system. It has the largest number of students, the greatest number of world-class universities, and a higher proportion of students in the STEM fields (science, technology, engineering, and mathematics) [6].

Twenty universities in Asia (not including Australia) have risen into the ranks of the world's top 200 universities, a pace which could see a fifth of the top 200 universities become Asia-based by 2040 [7, 8]. It is no surprise that international cooperation in higher education has become a significant strategy for Asia. Asian university presidents are globally engaged in an assortment of consortia, such as the Association of Pacific Rim Universities, World University Network, U21, Asia University Alliance and similar associations. The proportion of non-local academic staff in Asia has climbed, especially in Hong Kong. The University of Hong Kong in Southern China has the highest proportion of international academic staff of any comprehensive research university in the world [9]. China also has the third highest number of foreign students after the USA and UK.

2 New Center of International Cooperation

Eastern Asia has become the most attractive region for international cooperation in higher education. Countries like Japan, the Republic of Korea, Singapore, China, including the Chinese societies of Hong Kong, Macao, and Taiwan have a recognized tradition that highly values education. Along with its neighboring countries, the region has some of the most talented human resources in the world. Most economies of eastern Asia are market-oriented. Many of its political systems are liberal democracies. In eastern Asia, only the People's Republic of Korea is extraordinarily oppressive and orders assassinations of its enemies.

There are several reasons why Asia has become a center for international cooperation in higher education. National borders have become less relevant than in the past. Asia has excellent global telecommunications and a free international flow of funds. There is also a substantial transnational flow of commerce, communications, and ideas that are supranational and operate beyond the effective reach of governments. Even as boundaries become more porous and permeable, there is growing acceptance of the view that international collaboration in higher education, if done well, can be mutually beneficial on multiple levels. There is a recognition that the intensified international sharing of ideas, strategies of learning, and exchange of students can be of enormous value to systems and institutions and at the same time, it is also essential for improving the quality of teaching and research. To this end, Asia has the motivation, goal orientation, infrastructure, and record of efficient outcomes associated with international collaboration in higher education [10].

G. A. Postiglione (✉)
The University of Hong Kong, Pok Fu Lam, Hong Kong
e-mail: gerry@hku.hk

© The Author(s) 2020
A. AI-Youbi et al. (eds.), *Successful Global Collaborations in Higher Education Institutions*,
https://doi.org/10.1007/978-3-030-25525-1_4

3 Regional Partnership Within International Cooperation

Economic globalization has made it more urgent for Asia to consider how its long-term success may become dependent upon its ability to constitute itself as a regional block in the same way as the European Union [11]. It already acknowledges shared cultural traditions, historical affinities, and developmental experiences. As it becomes a more regionally integrated economic system and comprehensive free trade zone, it will consider regionally convertible educational credentials across colleges and universities. Such a trend would have broad implications for wider international cooperation.

While Asia's cultural, and especially linguistic and religious, diversity exceeds that found on other continents, there are shared themes. These include harmony, moral cultivation, social networks, and paternal leadership. These themes continue even while there is a strengthening of civil societies in Asia. The pre-colonial era is increasingly viewed as a time of free trade amid harmonious interchange. For most countries, colonialism affected statehood and forms of governance, as well as language, schooling, and especially higher education. While colonialism intensified cross-national difference, its education systems led to a convergent form of schooling.

The surge of Asian values discourse of the 1980s and 1990s was tempered by the economic crisis that transitioned the region into the twenty-first century. In the Southeast, Association of Southeast Asian Nations (ASEAN) has sustained itself as a symbol of regional identity and mutual respect. In the Northeast, the complex historical legacies of the twentieth century have not slowed the economic rise of China, South Korea, and Japan, who share an intimate cultural and educational heritage. These two Asian power centers, North and South, have intensified their educational interchange and cooperation, with China playing an increasing role in attracting students from other Asian countries. With a vast landmass that spans North and South and borders with 16 countries, China has espoused a vision of shared prosperity and harmony across the vast lands of its ancient Silk Road and Maritime Road. China's one-party system practices Leninist governance supplemented by Confucian values. While it does not aim to export its system of governance, it eschews Western values and places a premium on social stability, economic development, and a greater role in world affairs [12].

4 Asian Aspirations for World-Class Standards in Higher Education

East Asia's aspirations are reflected in the plans of its national leaders, education ministers, and university presidents. They include calling for the building of world-class universities and are backed by excellence initiatives. These include, for example, China's 211, 985, and Double First Class (*shuang yiliu*) programs, Japan's Doyama Plan, and South Korea's Brain Korea 21 [13, 14]. A number of flagship universities in Hong Kong and Singapore have attained world-class standards. Malaysia aims to do the same. Top-tier universities repackage cultural heritage within a shifting international geopolitical context toward fulfilling the penultimate Asian aspiration—to be the major sphere of global prosperity in the second half of the twenty-first century.

Even with diverse religious and ideological orientations and rapid socio-political transitions, Asian societies, with few exceptions, are noted for executive-led governance, consensus-driven management styles, and gradual but steady progress to democratize within slowly incubating civil societies [15, 16].

A major challenge for international cooperation is that higher education development across Asia is still highly uneven, both within and across countries. Massification has placed added pressure on the higher education systems to promote innovative thinking within the volatile global environment of competitive market economies [17, 18]. Asian universities are stereotyped as less able than Western universities to promote creative thinking. Thus, international cooperation is sometimes viewed as a way to foster more innovative methods of teaching and learning in university.

International university partnerships are also a way to build strategies to offset demographic effects by attracting international students and deepening international alliances. The average fertility rates in Singapore, South Korea, Japan, and Taiwan are only 1.3. The fertility rate in Hong Kong, where there are no restrictions on the number of children, are as low as in the Chinese mainland where policy permits only one child per household. At the other end of the spectrum are Asian countries like Malaysia, the Philippines, Nepal, Thailand, Bangladesh, Pakistan, and India where the fertility rates rise above 2.1 [19]. This points to the growing importance of international student flows within Asia and across the globe.

The time is ripe to explore some of the fundamental issues in international cooperation in higher education and how they have been shaped by historical experiences [20]. Macroscopic themes such as globalization, decentralization, and privatization continue to plow their way across the landscape of discourse about how to reform university governance [21, 22]. How Asia comes to reconcile these themes has been a formidable area for exploration [23, 24].

The full potential of international cooperation for eastern Asia continues to unfold. This process is still in its infancy, and it would be premature to project its long-term outcome. One should not ignore how international cooperation in higher education is shaped to some extent by socio-historical contexts that include cultural traditions, colonial experiences, and postcolonial transformations, all culminating in a set of new pressures affecting the roles and strategies of higher education systems and institutions.

5 Emerging Trends in International Cooperation

The forces that have fueled greater international collaboration provide a starting point in this exploration of new roles and strategies. Among the most dramatic developments across Asia are the rapid expansion and diversification of higher education systems and the increased prominence being given to higher education within national development plans. This prominence is due largely to the convergence of five trends within the region: (a) changing demographics, (b) the success of many countries in expanding access and raising the quality of their primary and secondary education systems, (c) increased integration among countries driven by economic globalization, (d) the shift from product-based to knowledge-based economies, and (e) improved communication and technological acceleration. In responding to these factors, higher education institutions have been confronted with new demands for access, quality, economic self-sufficiency, transparency, and relevance. Many institutions have responded with creative programs and strategies. There is an imperative to search for relevant and cost-effective approaches for juggling the competing demands of their multiple audiences.

5.1 Changing Demographics

Demand for higher education across Asia has grown rapidly and will continue to grow [4, 5, 25, 26]. Demand is influenced by the size of the school-age population, primary and secondary school participation and completion rates, rising family incomes, cultural traditions, willingness of urban households to invest in higher education, and a more competitive labor market. The pattern across the majority of countries is that more students are entering general education, a higher percent are finishing secondary school, and an increasing proportion of those graduates wants to continue to higher education.

However, there is rising concern about an increase in graduate unemployment in countries with systems of mass higher education. In China, Japan, and South Korea, higher education enrollments will drop as the number of secondary school graduates shrinks. In Japan and South Korea, the number of college enrollment places is about the same as the annual number of secondary school graduates. With eight million college and university graduates per year, China is concerned about unemployment. In Japan and Singapore, where graduate unemployment is low, governments are pressed to consider importing talent and specialized personnel from other countries. Both Japan and Singapore look to mainland China and other neighboring countries with an eye to recruiting students who will sign on to short- and long-term work contracts after graduation.

5.2 Success in Expanding Access to Primary and Secondary Education

East Asian nations have been enormously successful in popularizing nine years of basic schooling. Most countries have been willing to invest heavily in basic education and, with the exception of the top-tier universities, leave the bulk of higher education to the private sector. The notable exceptions have been Singapore and Hong Kong but even there, this situation is changing as more privatization takes hold.

The remarkable success of many countries across eastern Asia in expanding access to primary and secondary schooling is now fueling a sharply increased social demand for access to higher education opportunities. This demand is understandable and unstoppable. Primary and secondary schools provide students with a grounding in basic literacy, numeracy, and other vital skills while higher education offers the depth and flexibility people need to thrive in the modern workplace [27].

Given the important role highly educated people play in social and economic development, investment in higher education is viewed in the public interest. The issue is not primary and secondary education versus higher education but achieving the right mix among the three levels. Having willingly saddled up to the global discourse on the knowledge economy, Asian countries have opened a variety of channels beyond primary and secondary schooling to what was formerly the higher elite sector of the education system. Many countries, notably China and South Korea, are even willing to risk student unrest by such a massive expansion of higher education.

5.3 Economic Integration

Increased economic interdependency among countries, the speed of communications and the increasing importance of technology in business and government have created new demands for higher level technical, managerial, and administrative skills. Evidence consistently shows that countries that invest heavily in higher education benefit economically and socially from that choice. For example, research has found that in Organization for Economic Cooperation and Development (OECD) countries, every dollar invested in attaining high-skilled qualifications results in getting even more money back through economic growth [28]. This investment provides tangible benefits to all of society, not just the individuals who benefit from the greater educational opportunities. It is reasonable to assume that, in the robust economies of East Asia, a similar pattern would hold true.

While most Asian countries engage in increased economic globalization and are willing to enter a phase of mass higher education, they are apprehensive about taking on what is a formidable financial burden, especially for developing countries like Vietnam, Malaysia, and Thailand. There is little choice for such nations to not only begin charging fees but also to strongly support the private sector's move into widespread fee-paying higher education. Before long, this becomes a part of international cooperation with many Western universities setting up shop in Asia by establishing campuses or pairing with local universities to offer new and innovative degree programs.

5.4 Shift to Knowledge-Based Economies

International finance, business management, and national governance increasingly depend on automation, high-speed communication, and complex information flows that require administrative sophistication, technical proficiency, and analytic capacity. Secondary education alone cannot provide the needed managerial and technical leadership for modern business, industry, and government. Moreover, economic and social development increasingly depends upon innovation that universities have a potentially important role in fostering. Universities can do this through their role in carrying out research and development and by training workers for the knowledge economy [3, 29]. There is a widespread view in Asia that the ability to innovate is crucial in order to be globally competitive and that the university systems of the West have done far better in this respect. Thus, international higher education programs become scaffolds to bridge the innovativeness divide.

5.5 Improved Communication Systems

Improved communication systems have revolutionized international commerce in many areas. Information about new products and services, competitive product pricing, and user satisfaction are instantly available and can be widely shared. These communication systems have allowed Asian countries to advertise their programs to potential students, deliver online courses to students otherwise unable to access a campus, and foster collaboration among researchers across widely dispersed universities. Cooperation and competition

among higher education systems are no longer constrained by weak communications. Some countries have tried to hold back the tide by close monitoring of international information flows. This has been less the case for educational courses and programs and more the case for ideas and academic dialog. While countries have largely been unsuccessful in stopping such issue-based academic exchanges, they continue to try.

While demand for higher education is still rising, higher education systems across the region are expanding chaotically. Many public institutions suffer from under-funding, lack of vision, poor management, and low morale. While many countries have increased their public expenditure on education, some, like Thailand, have decreased it. Most of Asia is below the recommended six percent expenditure of gross domestic product on education, including China, which has hovered near three to four percent. Malaysia, with over five percent of GDP going to education, towers above the rest. At the same time, low-quality private institutions have proliferated with little effective quality control [26].

A key reason for the low quality is that, during the rapid system expansion that has characterized the region, the demand for qualified college and university academic staff outstripped supply. This shortage has been exacerbated by the ever-increasing alternative employment opportunities for highly educated personnel within the growing economies of the region. Many institutions lack the resources to pay salaries that are competitive with private sector opportunities available to would-be faculty members. They also face the related challenge of holding the attention and loyalty of those instructional staff they do hire. Many faculty hold supplemental employment which competes for the time they would otherwise commit to their teaching and research. Nevertheless, there are indications that locally produced doctorates in some leading Asian economies are competitive with overseas returnees in terms of academic productivity [30].

5.6 Quality

The quality of higher education institutions is a pervasive concern in many Asian counties, a situation created, in part, by rapid system growth without sufficient attention to the conditions needed for success. Efforts to address concerns about quality have often involved international collaborations. These collaborations have often focused on developing faculty competence in content and pedagogy, the direct transfer of academic programs, and assistance in designing and implementing quality assurance programs. However, there is no mistaking the aspirations shared by several East Asian systems to have world-class universities and governments, notably Singapore, China, South Korea, and Japan.

Malaysians have shown their willingness to provide the finances necessary to propel their flagship institutions further ahead in the international rankings. Moreover, international strategies are assessed by flagship institutions as playing a key role in "knowing the competition."

5.7 Relevance

Two central aspects of relevance in Asia concern the extent that the knowledge and skills of secondary school graduates are aligned with the entrance requirements of higher education institutions and the extent that the knowledge and skills of higher education graduates are aligned with the labor market [31]. Some countries face problems at both points. International collaborations provide a means through which institutions can see how counterparts in other countries have addressed these issues and can obtain the expertise needed to address these issues in their own context.

One of the more prominent international trends affecting universities has been the call of governments and the private sector for colleges and universities to increase the relevance of the education they offer and the research they conduct. This is being felt across all dimensions of scholarship and one of the most visible manifestations has been in the weakening of traditional disciplinary boundaries. Academic staff are being challenged to make their research more multi- and interdisciplinary. Pragmatic traditions in business and commerce, emergent civil societies, and dependency on international economic trends act together to ensure that relevance embeds itself in the guiding discourse of universities. In Asian higher education, there has been a steady emphasis on skill-based higher education, especially higher technical and vocational education, to counter concerns about relevance.

In many Asian countries, higher education institutions grapple with a tension between aligning their entrance standards and curriculum to be responsive to students' prior level of learning versus aligning their curriculum to international standards. Higher education institutions that focus too heavily on trying to meet international quality expectations are pressured to divert resources to provide remediation and sometimes incur extremely high dropout rates as poorly prepared students are unable to do university-level work. The articulation between secondary and higher education requirements is further complicated in some countries by the responsibility for these levels of education being split between a ministry of education and a ministry of higher education. If communication between ministries is weak, the alignment of the curriculum and the accuracy of expectations tend to suffer.

Even as demand builds for greater access to higher education, graduates in some Asian countries have difficulty finding employment. In some cases, this is due to employers'

concerns about the quality of the education students received. In other cases, it is because students had only limited information about existing and projected employment opportunities, entry points for access to desired careers, and career ladders associated with desired professions. Some higher education institutions, such as Cantu University in Vietnam, have undertaken graduate tracer studies and employer surveys as a basis for assessing the relevance of their curriculum and instruction methods. Many other higher education institutions also benefit from doing so. China, in particular, is paying greater attention to improving services directed at more successful rates of graduate employment.

5.8 Access and Equity

Given the growing importance of higher education in Asia, there is a higher expectation about the rate of economic return to individuals with a college or university credential. It is important that opportunity be fairly distributed. While considerable progress has been made over the last decade, disparities surrounding gender, ethnicity, urban/rural residence, and income disparities continue to block access. As access across social categories rises, institutional stratification creates inequity. While the rate of rural students' access to higher education increases, their representation in top-tier universities remains low or decreases. This is also true for opportunities in overseas higher education.

Some societies prefer sending sons rather than daughters far away from home. In the case of students from ethnic minority regions in China, Vietnam, and elsewhere in Asia, many learn through their native language while learning the national language, but they must also learn English (or another foreign language) if they are to gain access to study overseas. Growing inequity in higher education distorts the distribution of benefits to society and impedes inclusive economic and social development.

6 Rapid Growth in Private Higher Education and International Cooperation

One of the most important implications for international cooperation in Asian higher education is the growth of the private sector. Across Asia, more than 35% of higher education students enroll in the private sector, and almost 60% of the region's Higher Educations Institutions (HEIs) are private. Government promotion of private providers in higher education and the growth of private higher education are much more significant in Asia than in other regions of the world [26].

In China, for example, expansion would be untenable without private higher education. Private providers relieve financial pressure on the government and provide more opportunities to those who can pay for a higher education. In 2002, there were 320,000 undergraduates studying in private colleges and universities, accounting for only 2.2% of all China's undergraduates. By 2006, there were 318 private independent colleges enrolling 1,467,000 students. In 2016, there were 1861 public and 734 private institutions of higher education. The total revenue of private higher education increased from 69.6 billion rmb to 95.4 billion rmb from 2012 to 2016. It represented 9.6% of all the revenue of Chinese higher education and is expected to increase to 139 billion rmb in the future. The number of students in private higher education increased from 5.3 million in 2012 to 6.3 million in 2016 and represents 22% of all students in higher education. The number is expected to reach nearly eight million by 2021 (24% of all students) [32].

Indonesia has 4274 higher education institutions, most of which are private [33, 34]. Malaysia, the Philippines, Thailand, and Vietnam are moving in the same direction [35–37]. The increase in private sector involvement has raised the issue about pubic good versus private goods. It becomes less of an issue if the government implements proper regulatory mechanisms for effective quality assurance. Systems are needed to monitor and guarantee that the higher education provided by both public and private institutions meets quality standards. Quality assurance also ensures that all students, including those from disadvantaged groups, have equal access to higher education, whether public or private. Governments alone cannot provide enough higher education opportunities, but they can make policies and create strategies for monitoring the quality and standards of educational programs launched through international cooperation.

Each Asian country has its own regulations for international cooperation. In Malaysia, international service providers must have a physical presence. This ensures the provider's legal liability within Malaysia. The European Union (EU) frameworks such as the Bologna Declaration for higher education have become somewhat of a model for academic higher education in the same way as the European Training Framework is for Technical and Vocational Education and Training (TVET). These provide a way to view international program structure and credit transfer. However, implementation in Asia is a greater challenge. The government may regulate the market, but sufficient incentives are essential to encourage wider provision. Government subsidies can be strategically employed to incentivize providers toward rural and remote communities.

Among the options to strengthen human resource capacity are (1) using government funds, such as the Nazarbayev University in Kazakhstan (2) developing partner initiatives such as the Korea International Cooperation Agency with Uzbekistan that focuses on higher technical and vocational education (3) Indonesia's partnering with the Asian Development Bank to target polytechnic colleges, and (4) the Asian Development Bank and Vietnam's partnering initiative to strengthen the quality of universities [25].

7 International Cooperation Amid a Concern About Sovereignty

As China's leadership around the world has grown, its university system has become increasingly engaged internationally. Hundreds of Sino-foreign joint ventures in higher education on Chinese soil were approved. Hundreds of Confucian Institutes for the study of Chinese language and culture were established by the Chinese government on foreign soil. There are plans to establish two Chinese university campuses overseas, one in Seattle, USA and one in Malaysia. The number of international students coming to China continues to rise, and the number of Chinese self-funded students leaving for overseas continues to grow. Many who go overseas to study do not return, though the number of returnees is on the rise as China's economy opens new job opportunities.

By 2013, there were 1060 approved Sino-foreign joint ventures in higher education with 450,000 students involved. Since 2003, there have been 1,050,000 from higher education institutions [38]. Sino-foreign cooperation in higher education comes with stern warnings about risks to Chinese sovereignty, as a minister of education remarked: "Tough tasks lie ahead for China to safeguard its educational sovereignty as it involves our fundamental political, cultural, and economic interests and every sovereign nation must protect them from being harmed" [39]. Thus, the debate about liberal studies and science education is inseparable from the debate about the establishment of international cooperation. The issue remains embedded within an unambiguous paradox, namely the difficult compatibility of three elements within its university system: internationalization, institutional autonomy, and educational sovereignty.

The 2003 law on educational joint ventures opened the floodgates to hundreds of partnerships between Chinese and foreign universities. Reforms are underway at top Chinese universities to adapt and innovate on models of liberal higher education customary abroad. Attention is building about whether foreign-partnership campuses can have a significant impact on China's current higher education system. These collaborations and partnerships constitute one type of laboratory for innovative formats in higher learning. While the jury remains out on the long-term sustainability of international campuses, both host and guest universities will learn a great deal from cooperation in the running of partnered colleges and universities [40].

The majority of international university programs are taught and run by foreign academics, at a substantial premium, within Chinese universities. They are popular with middle-class parents because they give their children the cachet of a foreign education without the cost of studying abroad. In a few cases, foreign universities have gone one step further and set up full campuses with Chinese universities. Nottingham University has a campus in Ningbo; Shanghai Jiaotong and the University of Michigan run an engineering institute in Shanghai; and Xi'an Jiaotong and Liverpool University have established an independent university in Suzhou, among others. In 2013, New York University, which already has overseas study programs in ten countries, opened a new campus in Shanghai with East China Normal University. It will conduct integrated classes in humanities and social sciences, with an equal number of Chinese and foreign students. Duke University has also established a campus in Kunshan in partnership with Wuhan University. Keane University, the only one that is part of a state university system in the US, has established a campus in Wenzhou.

The rise in Sino-foreign joint ventures has led to more discussion about sovereignty in higher education. An influential scholar of Chinese higher education cautions that permitting foreign entities to hold a majority (more than 51%) of institutional ownership can lead to an "infiltration of Western values and cultures at odds with current Chinese circumstances" [41]. The Vice-Director of the Shanghai Education Commission makes it clear that a Sino-foreign venture in running an educational institute has to "make sure China's sovereignty and public interests are not harmed" [42]. To do so, at least half of its board of directors have to be Chinese citizens. A Ministry of Education official pointed out that China's commitment to providing access to its educational market is larger than any other developing country and therefore, "we must safeguard China's educational sovereignty, protect national security, and guide such programs in the right direction" [43]. Nevertheless, foreign campuses have been having an increased amount of autonomy with less interference from the host campuses since the 2003 law on Sino-foreign cooperation. However, they must still adhere to regulations set out by provincial level education bureaus who exert substantial control over student admission and financial issues.

International collaboration provides a mechanism through which universities can access international models for promoting access and equity. In the case of China, the breakneck-paced expansion is clear as only four percent of the 18–22 age group was involved in higher education in 1995 but had increased by 2018 to surpass 45%.

Inevitably, universities that seek to improve their quality will need to internationalize. Some institutions view international programs as both a way of creating an incentive for their faculty's improvement and a way of securing technical assistance in capacity development.

While international cooperation can involve different dimensions of the university's mission, one of the largest is in the provision of academic programs. Within East Asia, China is somewhat unique in its role as *both* an importer and exporter of higher education.

8 Conclusion: The Inevitability of International Cooperation

Asian knowledge systems will increasingly hinge upon the speed, depth, breadth, and changing nature of international cooperation in higher education. The northeast Asian countries of Japan, South Korea, and China with embedded cultural traditions of post-confucianism already have flagship universities that are considered world class. Southeast Asia, being far more diverse in terms of cultural traditions, as well as experiences with colonialism and statehood, has encased their universities in the global discourse of knowledge economics. Singapore leads the region in the global ranking of its universities and Malaysia has taken major steps to introduce excellence initiatives.

For a variety of reasons, East Asia is becoming a major international competitor in science and technology. Zakaria's *Post-American World and the Rise of the Rest* [44] is a theme that is reflected in China's rapid economic upsurge. With more students in higher education, more world-class universities, and a higher proportion who choose to study STEM fields than in the USA, China has become increasingly influential among developing countries in Asia. The manner in which it internationalizes and engages with the rest of the world will greatly determine Asia's future. An international survey about the advantages of internationalization has revealed that universities are not only considering the benefits for students but also for both the universities and their societies. There is increased value being placed on enhancing international cooperation for building capacity and enhancing the quality of teaching and learning. This suggests the saliency of the view that internationalization is much more than a way of improving the quality of higher education. It also has a significantly positive effect on society [45].

Acknowledgements University Grants Committee, Research Grants Council of Hong Kong, project HKU 37600514. With appreciation to David Chapman, a former co-collaborator on Asian cross-border research in higher education, and a world-leading researcher in comparative education policy. I would also like to thank Qin Yunyun for her assistance.

References

1. ADB. (2017). *Investing in education in the Asia-Pacific region in the future: A strategic education sector study*. Manila: Asian Development Bank.
2. ADB. (2018). *Asian development outlook*. Manila: Asian Development Bank.
3. ADB. (2018). *Strategy 2030: Achieving a prosperous, inclusive, resilient, and sustainable Asia and the Pacific*. Manila: Asian Development Bank.
4. ADB. (2010). *Education by 2020*. Manila: Asian Development Bank.
5. ADB. (2010). *Higher education across Asia: An overview of issues and strategies*. Manila: Asian Development Bank.
6. Woetzel, J., Chen, Y., Manyika, J., Roth, E., Seong, J., & Lee, J. (2015). The China effect on global innovation. *McKinsey Global Institute Research Bulletin*. http://www.mckinseychina.com/wp-content/uploads/2015/07/mckinsey-china-effect-on-global-innovation-2015.pdf. Accessed on February 7, 2019.
7. Times Higher Education. World university rankings 2018. https://www.timeshighereducation.com/world-university-rankings/2018/world-ranking#!/page/0/length/25/sort_by/rank/sort_order/asc/cols/stats. Accessed on February 7, 2019.
8. Postiglione, G. A. (2015, April 27). Asian universities are rising in the ranks. *The Washington Post*.
9. Postiglione, G. A., & Jung, J. (2017). *The changing academic profession in Hong Kong: Governance, productivity, and global integration*. Cham, Switzerland: Springer.
10. Altbach, P. A., & Umakashi, T. (Eds.). (2004). *Asian universities: Historical perspectives and contemporary challenges*. Baltimore: Johns Hopkins University Press.
11. ADB. (2008). *Emerging Asian regionalism: A partnership for shared prosperity*. Manila: Asian Development Bank.
12. Tsang, S. (2019, February 7). The West needs to better understand Xi Jinping thought as China becomes more formidable. *South China Morning Post*.
13. Postiglione, G. A., & Arimoto, A. (2015). Asia's research universities. *Higher Education, 70*(2).
14. Huang, F. (2017, September 29). Double world-class project has more ambitious aims. *University World News*.
15. Watson, J. (2004). Globalization in Asia: Anthropological perspectives. In M. Suárez-Orozco & D. B. Qin-Hilliard (Eds.), *Globalization: Culture and education in the new millennium* (pp. 141–172). Berkeley: University of California Press.
16. Henders, S. J. (Ed.). (2004). *Democratization and identity: Regimes and ethnicity in East and Southeast Asia*. Lanham: Lexington Press.
17. Shin, J. C., Postiglione, G. A., & Huang, F. T. (2015). *Mass higher education development in East Asia: Strategy, quality, and challenges*. Cham, Switzerland: Springer.
18. Suárez-Orozco, M., & Qin-Hilliard, D. B. (Eds.). (2004). *Globalization: Culture and education in the new millennium*. Berkeley: University of California Press.
19. Yip, P. (2019, January 9). Quality not quantity. *South China Morning Post*.
20. Cummings, W. K. (2003). *The institutions of education: A comparative study of education development in the six core nations*. Oxford: Symposium Books.
21. Mok, K. H. (Ed.). (2004). *Centralization and decentralization: Educational reforms and changing governance in Chinese societies*. Netherlands: Springer Press.
22. Bjork, C. (2006). *Educational decentralization: Asian experiences and conceptual contributions*. Netherlands: Springer Press.
23. Mok, K. H. (2006). *Education reform and education policy in East Asia*. London: Routledge.
24. Postiglione, G. A., & Tan, J. T. H. (2007). *Going to school in East Asia at school*. New York: Greenwood Press.
25. ADB. (2012). *Regional cooperation and cross-border collaboration*. Manila: Asian Development Bank.
26. ADB. (2012). *Private higher education across Asia: Expanding access, searching for quality*. Manila: Asian Development Bank.
27. Task Force on Higher Education and Society. (2000). *Higher education in developing countries: Peril and promise*. Washington D.C.: World Bank.
28. Schleicher, A. (2006). *The economics of knowledge: Why education is key for Europe's success*. Brussels: The Lisbon Council.
29. LaRocque, N. (2007). *The role of education in supporting the development of science, technology and innovation in developing member countries*. Manila.
30. Shin, J. S., Jung, J., Postiglione, G., & Azman, N. (2014). Research productivity of returnees from study abroad in Korea, Hong Kong, and Malaysia. *Minerva: A Review of Science, Learning Policy, 52*(4), 467–487.
31. ADB. (2013). *Improving transitions: From school to university to workplace*. Manila: Asian Development Bank.
32. Yu, K. (2018). The consolidation of Chinese private higher education. *International Higher Education, *(95), 21–23.
33. Nizam, I. (2006). Indonesia: The need for higher education reform. In *Higher education in South-East Asia*. Bangkok: UNESCO Asia and Pacific Regional Bureau for Education.
34. Sukamoto. (2002). Private higher education in Indonesia. In UNESCO PROAP & SEAMO RIHED (Eds.), *The report of the second regional seminar on private higher education: Its role in human resource development in a globalized knowledge society*. Bangkok: UNESCO RIHED.
35. LaRocque, N. (2002). *Private education in the Philippines: A market and regulatory survey*. Manila: Asian Development Bank.
36. LaRocque, N. (2005). *Private partnerships in education: The case of the Philippines*. Washington, DC: World Bank.
37. Hayden, M., & Khanh, D. V. (2010). Private higher education in Viet Nam. In G. Harman, M. Hayden, & P. T. Nghi (Eds.), *Reforming higher education in Vietnam: Challenges and priorities*. Netherlands: Springer.
38. Lin, J. (Ed.). (2017). *Chinese-foreign cooperation in running schools: To improve quality, to serve the overall strategies and to enhance capability*. Xiamen: Xiamen University Press.
39. Chen, Z. L. (2002). The impact of WTO on China's educational enterprise and related policies. *People's Education, 3*, 4–7.
40. Wildavsky, B. (2012). *The great brain race: How global universities are reshaping the world*. Princeton, NJ: Princeton University Press.
41. Pan, M. (2009). An analytical differentiation of the relationship between education sovereignty and education rights. *Chinese Education and Society, 42*(4), 88–96.
42. Zhang, M. (2009). New era, new policy: Cross-border education and Sino-foreign cooperation in running schools in the eyes of a fence-sitter. *Chinese Education and Society, 42*(4), 23–40.

43. Zhang, L. (2009). Policy direction and development trends for Sino-foreign partnership schools. *Chinese Education and Society, 42*(4), 11–22.
44. Zakaria, F. (2009). *The post-American world and the rise of the rest*. New York: Penguin.
45. Maronini, G., Egron-Polak, E., & Green, M. (2019, February 1). A changing view of the benefits of HE internationalization. *University World News*.

Open Access This chapter is licensed under the terms of the Creative Commons Attribution 4.0 International License (http://creativecommons.org/licenses/by/4.0/), which permits use, sharing, adaptation, distribution and reproduction in any medium or format, as long as you give appropriate credit to the original author(s) and the source, provide a link to the Creative Commons license and indicate if changes were made.

The images or other third party material in this chapter are included in the chapter's Creative Commons license, unless indicated otherwise in a credit line to the material. If material is not included in the chapter's Creative Commons license and your intended use is not permitted by statutory regulation or exceeds the permitted use, you will need to obtain permission directly from the copyright holder.

Part II

International Collaboration and Knowledge Transfer

International Collaboration as a Catalyst for Change: The Case of Nanyang Technological University, Singapore 2003–2017

5

Guaning Su

1 Introduction

1.1 Genesis

I had the honour of serving as the second president of Nanyang Technological University (NTU) from 1 January 2003 to 30 June 2011. Following the end of my term, Professor Bertil Andersson, whom I had recruited in 2007 as the first Provost, continued our work as my successor. By the end of Andersson's term on 31 December 2017, we had engineered, together with Emeritus Professor Haresh Shah of Stanford University, an unprecedented transformation of a large university in a relatively short time of fifteen years. This transformation and a detailed account of how we did it are discussed in our new book under preparation [1].

I was a university president in a hurry from the first day of my presidency on the 1st of January, 2003. I began introducing initial reforms while carrying out the government decision to expand the university undergraduate enrolment by 6300 students. This was to be done by building three new schools in Humanities and Social Sciences, Art, Design and Media and Physical and Mathematical Sciences as part of the Singapore plan to expand the university sector. The granting of university autonomy as well as the establishment of the National Research Foundation of Singapore in 2006 provided the empowerment and the resources for a thorough revamp of the leadership and the faculty to meet the new research-intensive innovation requirements. From the beginning of my term on the 1st of January, 2003, until the end of Andersson's term on the 31st of December, 2017, the university experienced a quantum leap in international stature as a result of dramatic increases in research output and research quality. While rankings are incomplete measurements of universities, the magnitude of NTU's transformation can be seen from the 2020 Quacquarelli-Symonds (QS) World University Rankings [2] in which NTU now ranks joint 11th in the world.

In this chapter, I shall examine the role of globalisation in the transformation of NTU and argue that international resources can only serve as the catalyst. Sustainable transformation is not possible without meaningful and often painful internal reform. Because of this caveat, transformations such as we achieved in 15 years are still rare events in the chronicles of higher education.

1.2 Historical Background

NTU was founded as a practice-oriented engineering college named Nanyang Technological Institute (NTI) in 1981. It received its university charter by an Act of the Singapore Parliament [3] in 1991. Singapore has always looked upon the university as an instrument for economic growth. As a result, the Economic Development Board (EDB) has a major influence on manpower planning and higher education policy. As Singapore's economy continued to develop rapidly and the demand for engineers skyrocketed, NTI was created to answer this need. Between 1991 and 2002, NTU developed as a professionally focused university graduating engineers, executives, accountants and media professionals.

By 1999, Singapore's economic strategy had shifted towards research, innovation and entrepreneurship [4]. By 2003, when I took office, change was overdue. At a per capita GDP of roughly USD 50,000, Singapore faced an uphill task to ensure that our innovation and productivity gains kept pace with GDP growth.

As President NTU, I began engineering a major transformation of the university. International networks and collaboration played an important part. However, we cannot simply rely on an external party to strengthen our capabilities. Otherwise, the impact is gone as soon as the external party disengages. The impact of international collaboration

G. Su (✉)
Nanyang Technological University, Singapore, Singapore
e-mail: guaning@ntu.edu.sg

© The Author(s) 2020
A. Al-Youbi et al. (eds.), *Successful Global Collaborations in Higher Education Institutions*,
https://doi.org/10.1007/978-3-030-25525-1_5

was catalytic in that it provided the role model and advice. We still had to figure out how to overcome the natural human resistance and create a sustainable model of excellence. Here, the government, as the ultimate sponsor and customer of the university's output, played a crucial role. Fundamental internal reforms were necessary if the drive of the university was to create the necessary impact. This internal reform is the hardest part of a university's transformation and a focus of our forthcoming book [1].

1.3 Competitive Position

In 2002, before I took office, NTU was a regionally known and professionally focused teaching institution. My predecessor, Professor Cham Tao Soon, had written extensively on the 1981–2002 period in the NTU Story [5] and NTU Story Part II [6]. NTU was used to occupying the number 2 position in a comfortable duopoly with the National University of Singapore (NUS), but in 2003, it was in danger of dropping to number 3 in student preference. This risk arose with the entry of a smaller, livelier and Ivy League linked rival, Singapore Management University (SMU). SMU was set up in collaboration with the Wharton School at the University of Pennsylvania. There was a real danger of NTU ending up as number 3, scraping the bottom of the barrel in student intake quality. I had to take urgent action. Very quickly in February 2003, we announced NTU's move towards a flexible curriculum with many more choices of majors, minors and combinations thereof, which we branded as the New Undergraduate Experience. This event heralded the beginning of NTU's historic transformation. Teaching led the way.

At the time, NTU research was industry cooperation oriented. Top-level research was patchy. NTU had very little mindshare in top-level international research. I realised that simultaneous changes had to be made throughout the university. Eventually, it took not just one, but three high-powered individuals to achieve the ambitious goals I had in mind back in 2003. The outcome in 2018 was way beyond the expectations of the three of us.

1.4 Building the Team

As I was parachuted into the NTU presidency, it took me some time to get to know the people and more time to adjust the structure and develop a core team of like-minded leaders to drive the transformation. From 2003 to 2005, I tapped the existing university leadership to help out in the transformation. The result was mixed. Not all of them saw the need to change. Some did see the entry of the third university as a threat but were at a loss on what could be done. No one

worried about the economy passing us by and the need for research and innovation that we are duty-bound to provide but were unable to at the time.

The reforms stalled as we were bogged down with regular administrative issues. There were insufficient continuity and enforcement to push reforms on all fronts simultaneously. On the positive side, our drive to establish three new schools was making good progress, and all three were in operation by 2005.

2 Seizing the Opportunity

2.1 QAFU Review, Autonomous Universities and National Research Foundation

Fortunately, the opportunity for major reform came soon after this. The 2005 Quality Assurance Framework for Universities (QAFU) Review [7] endorsed our direction but was politely critical of the ad hoc nature of change. This supported the case I had been putting forward to move towards a provost structure, making the appraisal process inherited from the days as a government agency much more academic and transparent.

2.2 University Autonomy

The 2005 meeting of the Singapore Ministry of Education's International Academic Advisory Panel (IAAP) endorsed the Singapore Ministry of Education's proposal [8] to grant NUS and NTU autonomy, with a performance requirement and outcome-based funding, freeing our hands in fund-raising. I gratefully accepted the suggestion to recruit a provost with the utmost urgency and to build the university governance tapping well-established examples such as Stanford. The suggestion may have come from Gerhard Casper, President Emeritus of Stanford University, a member of the QAFU assessment panel.

2.3 National Research Foundation

Just as important as gaining autonomy and recruiting a provost was the establishment of the National Research Foundation (NRF) to provide strategic research funding within Singapore. In one stroke, the universities were freed to make proposals for grants from the NRF with single programme funding up to 150 M Singapore dollars, a mind-boggling sum at the time. This sum in turn gave the universities firepower to recruit the very best from around the world.

3 The Nanyang Troika

The recruitment of Bertil Andersson as Provost gave me a partner with vision who could be trusted to push our agenda with all his might. Haresh Shah was chair of the search committee. When Andersson signed his contract, our core team was complete. The third member of this Troika, Professor Haresh Shah, was a former department chair, entrepreneur and professor emeritus at Stanford. He was familiar with the system at Stanford and was keen to change NTU. He became a member of the Board of Trustees and chairman of the board-level Academic Affairs Committee. The Troika met for the first time in Aptos, California and brainstormed ten significant projects. After fifteen years of hard work, when Andersson stepped down in 2017, most of the targets had been achieved and validated externally. What happened between 2003 and 2017 was nothing short of miraculous.

By 2017, NTU Singapore was a highly regarded research-intensive university with a global reputation. We achieved our highest ever ranking at number 11 in the QS World University Rankings in 2017 and 2020. We were also the highest ranked Asian university in normalised research impact.

4 The Nature of Globalisation

As an important window to the world and a wellspring of ideas, not to mention the cradle of leaders, movers and shakers, the modern university cannot help but globalise. The nature and extent of globalisation differ between institutions because the mission of the university varies and evolves with time.

As already mentioned, NTU came into being as Nanyang Technological Institute (NTI) in 1981 on a campus bequeathed by its predecessor Nanyang University, a Chinese language university serving the Chinese community in South East Asia ("Nanyang" to the Chinese). NTI's founding mission in 1981 was to train large numbers of practice-oriented engineers for the Singaporean economy. Being chartered as NTU, a full-fledged university, in 1991, did not change the mission but broadened it to include educating professionals in accounting and business as well as mass communications. It was appropriate, with this mission, that globalisation had a practice rather than research focus. Some senior leaders even actively discouraged young colleagues from doing research on the premise that it was irrelevant to the university.

5 International Collaboration with Top Schools

5.1 The MIT Review

As the Singapore economy began to mature and achieve a high GDP per capita, this vacuum in research became a shortcoming. In 1997, the International Academic Advisory Panel was set up by the Singapore Ministry of Education. In 1998, the Ministry commissioned a team of professors from MIT to review NTU and sister institution National University of Singapore (NUS). The team recommended a change from the British style of narrow, but deep education towards a broad undergraduate curriculum and a renewed emphasis on research [9].

5.2 Singapore—MIT Alliance

A deal was struck with MIT to begin a major research collaboration between MIT, NUS and NTU. It was dubbed the Singapore—MIT Alliance (SMA). This was a clear signal from the government that world-class research was demanded for both NUS and NTU. SMA was a classic case of financial considerations being used to help establish somewhat unequal research collaboration. Of course, the disparity in capabilities cannot be too great or else meaningful collaboration would not be viable.

Looking back, the SMA programme was positioned well. SMA did not only raise the level of research in both NUS and NTU but also provided much needed affirmation that some of our faculty can match the best in the world. This confidence was an important prerequisite for the subsequent transformation of both universities.

5.3 SMART

It is important to keep in mind that globalisation is a many-to-many courtship dance. Contacts and mutual visits are used to size each other up. The relationship is normally polygamous. Deals are consummated all the time, just as some deals outlive their welcome and lapse. SMA served its purpose well. It's follow-up, SMART, where RT stands for research and technology was a collaboration on a more equal basis. Today, NUS and NTU, the two flagship universities in Singapore no longer require "foreign aid" programmes, but instead attract collaboration from peer institutions on an equal basis. In addition, both universities have now become attractive targets being wooed by others to help them raise their levels of research.

for some time with the lubrication of funds offered in compensation to the stronger partner, eventually, the weaker partner drops out because the gains do not justify the cost.

6 International Networks

Every university worth its salt is a node in a number of international networks of universities. This is a sweeping statement, but nonetheless true. Consider, first of all, the essential component of any university: the teaching faculty. Except for a very small number of bespoke institutions such as military academies, it is necessary to cast the recruitment net far and wide; in other words, a world-wide search is often best. This is globalisation on the fundamental professorial level.

What about the recruitment of students? A university typically has a student body drawn from many countries around the world. While those from the home country are always the dominant component, students in most countries around the world aspire to attend the best global universities wherever they are physically located. Whether their dream schools are in their home country is immaterial. Increasing affluence also allows them to broaden the scope of their search for the ideal university by going international.

6.1 Research Collaboration

The most globalised university activity is research. The broad themes of research tend to follow a global consensus and do not vary much country to country. There is considerable agreement among all countries on which are the most important problems facing mankind. It is also the nature of research that progress is incremental and often multinational. The more advanced university's research, the more important their international network is, often built by professors for particular big problems or grand challenges.

The topology of a university's international network is multidimensional. At the most fundamental level, it is a person-to-person relationship usually based on a shared research interest. Unsaid, but very important, is that the relationship must create a win–win situation. If the levels of research are too disparate, one side feels exploited and taken advantage of while the other side feels inferior and worse, looked down upon. Neither case leads to a sustainable relationship.

At the university-to-university level, relationships are an aggregate of individual relationships augmented by institutional links, typically in alliances and collaboration in joint teaching and research. At this level, the matching of capabilities is even more important. If there is a major gap in capabilities, even though collaboration can still be sustained

6.2 NTU Networks

NTU, too, had these multidimensional networks back in 2003 when I began to push its transformation. The networks were built up mainly for the 1981 mission of educating practice-oriented engineers and for foreign policy needs, such as those pertaining to the Association of Southeast Asian Nations (ASEAN). However, by 2003, these networks had become less relevant to serve the needs of a high income (and therefore high cost), innovation-based and high value-added economy where technological innovation is key to obtaining the necessary value added. For example, the Commonwealth Engineering Council (CEC), with participation from all former British colonies, was useful at the beginning of NTI to provide references on curriculum and linkages to multinational corporations. NTI even received accolades from the CEC for having developed one of the best engineering programmes in the world.

In 2003 when I assumed office, these links with largely teaching universities and industry employers of our graduates were dominant, taking up both resources and attention from management. I set out to develop international links that would be helpful for the progress of NTU in the context of the new demands of the nation, mainly on high-level research. Today, NTU's set of partners mostly come from the top tier of research universities.

6.3 Tapping Top Schools

Having worked with MIT in the SMA Programme since the late 1990s, MIT was a natural target. As I had a degree from Caltech and the Caltech presidential couple David Baltimore and Alice Huang were frequent visitors to Singapore by virtue of their engagement with the Agency for Science, Technology and Research (A*Star), the national research institute, these two top-rated technological powerhouses were attractive to engage. Of the two, I had more success with Caltech, partly because of alumni links, but also because MIT was quite content to let the relationship evolve naturally without too much pushing. Another success was our engagement with Stanford, the Silicon Valley powerhouse. It is interesting to see how these engagements with three of the very best tech schools turned out.

6.3.1 MIT

With MIT, besides the SMA programme, we had developed collaboration between our Nanyang Business School and

Sloan School of Management at MIT. This was the Nanyang Fellows programme, aiming to create a small and intimate environment for talented officials from the ASEAN region in an MBA-like programme. The aim was political—to develop early friendship among officials in ASEAN countries. Both the SMA programme and the Nanyang Fellows programme involved financial benefits for MIT. We were happy to pay the premium as both programmes benefitted the reputation and quality of two of our biggest schools, engineering and business. I visited MIT within a few months of taking office, but the meetings were more courtesy calls and reviews. MIT Provost Robert Brown was a long-serving member and Chairman of the IAAP where we can get in touch with him easily.

The next major move by MIT was the Singapore MIT Alliance on Research and Technology Programme within the Campus for Research and Technological Entrepreneurship (CREATE), where foreign universities of high standing were invited to set up research laboratories in Singapore. Of all the foreign universities in CREATE, MIT probably had the best deal with five programmes funded. NTU was not very involved. Overall, I would say NTU benefitted from MIT due to the good decisions from the incisive leadership of Robert A. Brown as Chairman of IAAP as well as because of the branding effect of participating in MIT led programmes.

6.3.2 Stanford

In 2003, I signed the Singapore–Stanford Partnership Agreement with President John Hennessy of Stanford. Background work on this agreement to collaborate on environmental engineering research and conduct master's and doctoral programmes was done by my predecessor. It was a typical agreement with a university with a higher overall research achievement and reputation. Stanford had the number 1 ranked environmental engineering programme. Environmental engineering was a specialised area of concentration in NTU and an area of emphasis in Singapore's research strategy. Thus, it was natural to offer financial inducements as sweeteners for collaboration. We must be aware, however, that the capability gap cannot be too large. No university want to have their top faculty bogged down bringing up someone else's faculty. It was a credit to NTU's environmental engineering faculty that Stanford saw it worth their while to collaborate, financial inducement or not.

During the course of my presidency, there were other occasions when we sought out Stanford as a partner. But the Stanford philosophy of tight control of their faculty quality meant that no other programme materialised. We did, however, through Haresh Shah, benefit from the Stanford experience as our governance framework concerning the Academic Council, the Senate, Senate Committees and the Advisory Committee were largely adapted from the ready-made systems at Stanford.

6.3.3 Caltech

NTU's relationship with Caltech was interesting and much deeper than the links with MIT or Stanford. Among my *alma maters,* I spent the least amount of time in Caltech as my Ph. D. programme was cut short by the Singapore government's insistence that I return to Singapore after completing my M. S. which I had finished in three quarters. I am most grateful to Caltech though, not only because I had a fellowship with no strings attached, but because a Caltech GPA of 4.0 opened many doors when I did resume applying for doctoral admissions.

Caltech also had a close relationship with the Singapore national research institutes, its president, Nobel laureate David Baltimore having struck up a relationship with the Chairman of A*Star, Philip Yeo, upon the launch of Singapore's ambitious biomedical initiative in 2000. David and his wife Alice Huang, a formidable scientist in her own right, were frequent visitors to Singapore. We were to become good friends. Philip Yeo invited Caltech to send a team to review NUS and NTU with a view towards establishing a new pharmaceutical chemistry programme. David Tirrell, then Head of the Chemistry and Chemical Engineering Division at Caltech, now provost, led the team.

At the time of the Caltech visit, NTU was just beginning to assemble the leadership for the new School of Physical and Mathematical Sciences while NUS had a strong and long-established chemistry department. The Caltech team recommended that A*Star establish the new chemistry programme in NTU where a fresh start was possible without any baggage from the past. I took a personal interest in the project as a Caltech alumnus, with the help of Freddy Boey, Chair of the School of Material Science and Engineering, and later Lee Soo Ying whom I recruited while he was on sabbatical at Berkeley after having stepped down from his Vice Provost position at NUS. Appointed Dean of Physical and Mathematical Sciences, he was a tremendous help to me in recruiting outstanding young faculty. Some of the recruits were from NUS which earned us howls of protest from their president.

What A*Star wanted was a strong pharmaceutical chemistry programme. Consistent with David Tirrell's findings, we set out to recruit young and promising faculty. To ensure good quality control, we proposed to recruit the young faculty jointly with Caltech and have them spend two years teaching and conducting research there before coming back to NTU. Obviously to make it worth their while, there were financial sweeteners for Caltech.

When we finally submitted what we thought was a winning proposal to A*Star, word came back that it was too expensive on a cost per Ph.D. graduated basis. But of course, this approach of building up faculty at the same time as students cost more. However, in the long run, it is more effective as we are building up our faculty at the same time as producing Ph.D.'s. Having world-class faculty is immeasurably more effective than sending groups of Ph.D. students to top schools.

What A*Star failed to take into account was the more important capability build-up in NTU research that would be a continuing source of high-quality Ph.D. graduates specific to industry requirements. Nevertheless, chemistry turned out to be one of our bright spots as we rose in stature and international reputation. Our relationship with Caltech helped significantly in the international exposure of our early recruits in 2004 which contributed to the prominence of NTU chemistry today.

6.4 Competing for Research Centres of Excellence (RCE)

Research Centres of Excellence were the flagship programmes of the NRF, each centre funded at SGD 150 M or about USD 120 M. There were to be five centres budgeted. Each centre would be affiliated with a university and spend their budget over 5–10 years. As NTU did not have a tradition of high-level research, we lacked the international network from which we could try to recruit top scientists to lead the programmes. Most people did not think NTU stood a chance competing with NUS and expected all five centres to be won by NUS.

We were in a precarious position. It was impossible to pull ourselves up by our bootstraps. Even with an external inject, Professor Tony Woo, Vice President (Research) recruited from the University of Washington, Seattle, the quality of NTU proposals that floated to the top were of insufficient quality.

We achieved a final tally of 3 for NUS, 2 for NTU. The two NTU wins were the Earth Observatory of Singapore (EOS) and the Singapore Centre for Environmental Life Sciences Engineering (SCELSE).

6.4.1 Earth Observatory of Singapore

An even more important effect of our relationship with Caltech led to NTU winning two major research competitions. The first one led to the establishment of the Earth Observatory of Singapore (EOS) at NTU. We were able, for the first time, to recruit a prominent Caltech professor, Kerry Sieh, to NTU, who helped us write the winning proposal. What stood out also was the willingness of Kerry to give up his Caltech position with life tenure and come to NTU full time which really means tenure to the age of 65. In light of the life tenure system in the USA, this was a tremendous sacrifice.

With Kerry at NTU, we had established in one stroke a world-class observatory of the natural and man-induced disasters in the South East Asia ring of fire, conducting research on earthquakes, tsunamis, volcanos and climate change due to global warming. Not only did this fill a vacuum in one of the hot spots of the world, but the close cooperation with local authorities in Singapore's neighbours also earned us considerable goodwill. For NTU, the award of the USD 120 M grant was a tremendous affirmation and morale booster. The significance of the EOS award goes beyond this. It demonstrated that NTU could hold its own in competition with NUS for these mega-grants and that we had the necessary creativity to chart our own path rather than compete where others had a head start. An immovable barrier had been breached, so to speak.

By this time, Jean-Lou Chameau had taken over from David Baltimore as President of Caltech. I knew Jean-Lou from his outstanding work at Georgia Tech where he was Dean of Engineering and later Provost, one of the triumvirate leadership at Georgia Tech responsible for their rapid rise in recent years. So, it was in friendly discussion with Jean-Lou that we applied the finishing touches to Kerry's move to NTU, including the price we paid for Kerry's tectonics movement instrumentation in Sumatra.

6.4.2 Singapore Centre for Environmental Life Sciences Engineering

There was one final touch by Caltech on NTU's research excellence. Jean-Lou Chameau had been invited as Caltech president to be a member of Singapore's IAAP. Next to the indefatigable Robert Brown, the President of Boston University, he was probably the most eloquent advocate of well-constructed and articulated research proposals. Our research proposal for the final round of the NRF's Research Centres of Excellence grant calls had everything. We proposed to establish the Singapore Centre for Environmental Life Sciences Engineering (SCELSE). Tapping the tremendous progress in genetic sequencing and inspired by gene-sequencing pioneer Craig Venter's voyage around the world to collect the genetic makeup of oceans, we proposed investing in the sequencing of microbial communities and developing engineering techniques to put them to use or to influence their behaviour. Not only would this effort create a new engineering discipline, it held out tremendous promise for environmental remediation and bodily infection intervention. Moreover, our Principal Investigators comprised not just NTU faculty and world-renowned authorities coming to NTU but also faculty in NUS, our local competitor. Rumour has it that this was the only proposal ever passed unanimously. Robert Brown and Jean-Lou Chameau's influence no doubt loomed large in such a deliberation. This move set up a collaboration model between the two Singaporean universities, often bitter rivals, creating a positive atmosphere of working for the national good.

6.5 National Research Foundation, Autonomous Universities and New Talent

Singapore's National Research Foundation made big resources available for competition by the major players, namely NUS, NTU and A*Star, the national research organisation. As autonomous universities, NUS and NTU became not-for-profit corporations, freed from the constraints of government processes and procedures. One particular outcome was the welcome ability to tailor compensation packages for exceptional academic talent. Coupled with the opportunity to win big research grants up to 120 M USD, this allowed both NUS and NTU to bring in exceptional senior faculty. Once the compensation barrier was breached, the horizon opened up suddenly for recruiting top talent at all levels including Assistant Professors.

In NTU, we created the Nanyang Assistant Professor (NAP) scheme in 2007 to bring in exceptional young talents through contact with the top laboratories around the world. Subsequent to NTU establishing the NAP scheme, the National Research Foundation set up the NRF Fellows scheme aimed at recruiting some of the best young principal investigators (PI) from around the world to Singapore. NTU worked hard to attract a fair share of the Fellows to NTU. The selection of the Fellows was entrusted to an international panel of prominent authorities in various areas of research and industry. I was the only Singaporean among them. We kept the work of the selection panel very low key to minimise lobbying problems.

NTU has had numerous collaboration programmes with international universities. These have tended to be specific programmes such as SMA with MIT, the Singapore-Stanford Partnership for environmental engineering and water treatment, Harvard Business School for our Asian Case Centre, and Carnegie Mellon for our M.Sc. in Financial Engineering. In each of these programmes, we learned something from the more advanced partner. We in turn are courted by many universities to collaborate with them, often with the backing of political relationships. Of all the foreign country relationships, the most important and most interesting is China.

6.6 China Programmes

Way back in 2003, when China's global influence was still small although growing rapidly, I had already determined that the engagement of China, tapping our Chinese speaking Nanyang University heritage, was a useful competitive strategy. We already had a head start with our so-called Mayor Class. This programme started in 1992 when paramount Chinese leader Deng Xiaoping suggested learning from Singapore. This was a one-year full-time Master programme taught in Chinese, aimed at educating Chinese senior officials in "Managerial Economics". This prepared them to manage market economies as required when China opened up with its reforms. It was dubbed the Mayor Class by the media as many of the officials became mayors of cities and beyond upon return to China. Building on the success of this programme, by the end of my term, we counted seven China-related master's programmes.

Besides the original Mayor Class, we added a more general Master of Public Administration, referring to both as Mayor Classes. The business school added an Executive Master of Business Administration, and the National Institute of Education added a Master's in Educational Administration. It was dubbed the Principal's Class. The Nanyang Technopreneurship Centre added a Master in Technopreneurship and Innovation. The Business School added a Master of Finance. Later, when the Central Organisation Department of the Chinese Communist Party issued an edict prohibiting party cadres from obtaining a foreign degree on government time and expense, our focus shifted to short-term courses and younger candidates and officials under different jurisdiction such as those from uniformed services and corporations.

As a result of these efforts, NTU has today over 20,000 senior-level alumni in China spread over all 35 provincial-level entities. A degree-conferring convocation ceremony has been held in China with all the pomp and circumstance of the home campus every year, at which the evening is devoted to building alumni relations and networks.

The impact of this important alumni network is yet to be fully felt, but with China jostling with the USA for world leadership, it will have an important, although as yet undetermined, impact on NTU, Singapore and the South East Asian region. The positive influence of NTU's China programmes on Singapore–China relationships has been, however, quite clear.

7 Conclusion

In this chapter, I have used the NTU example to illustrate how the Troika, itself a result of international relationships, was able to tap international collaboration to make possible the quantum leap at NTU. At first glance, one may attribute this to our globalisation efforts.

The benefits of globalisation are twofold. First, it provides good reference points to illustrate what is possible, and then it demonstrates the kind of actions necessary to do better. The reforms must initiate the right kind of behaviour; while at the right time, the system must lock in the desired changes.

Ultimately, the reforms at NTU were successful because we seized the opportunity and put in place mechanisms to keep and sustain the gains. For this, we attribute the achievement to the Troika, subject of a coming book on the rise of NTU being written by the three of us.

7.1 The Role of Globalisation in the Transformation of NTU

I had a wide-ranging globalised exposure in my education and work experience prior to coming to NTU. My undergraduate and postgraduate studies stretched over three countries—Singapore, Canada and the USA. My *Alma Mater* comprises five universities: the University of Alberta, Caltech, Singapore, Stanford and Harvard. My work experience in defence research also helped build me up to an international level that led to collaboration with Sweden, France, Australia, the UK and the USA. As serendipity would have it, while the search for the second NTU President was taking place, I was at Stanford studying the Silicon Valley entrepreneurship ecosystem. Not only did I get to know Haresh Shah there, but my links with Stanford and the Silicon Valley turned out to be very useful in the globalisation journey of NTU.

NTU's strong international relationships were further enhanced when we led the way in the formation of the Global Alliance of Technological Universities (GlobalTech), inaugurated in 2009 with seven universities across three continents. The alliance was formed on the basis of a common pursuit by these seven technological universities to improve the human condition and bring benefits to mankind, employing the technologies available. The founding members were Imperial College London, ETH Zurich, Caltech, Georgia Tech, IIT Bombay, Shanghai Jiao Tong, and NTU. The alliance is useful for branding ourselves with these top institutions.

From a position in the wilderness, Nanyang Technological University (NTU) has risen rapidly. The university is ranked joint 11th in the 2020 QS World University Rankings. Although international collaboration played an important part in this transformation, its influence is in surprising and non-traditional areas. It is easy to overestimate the importance of globalisation as it is a convenient scapegoat to blame for failure. The fundamental reason for NTU's rise is entirely internal.

References

1. Su, G., Andersson, B., & Shah, H. (in preparation). *The Nanyang Troika*. World Scientific: Singapore.
2. Quacquerelli-Symonds World University Rankings, 2020. https://www.topuniversities.com/university-rankings/world-university-rankings/2020. Accessed July 28, 2019.
3. Nanyang Technological University Act, Cap. 192, Singapore Statutes 1991, revised 9th March, 1992.
4. Ng, E. H., et al. (2003). *Restructuring the university sector—More opportunities, better quality*. Report of the Committee to Review the University Sector and Graduate Manpower Planning. Singapore: Ministry of Education.
5. Lu-Sinclair, Y. T. (1995). NTU book. In *The NTU story—The making of a university of industry and business*. Singapore: Nanyang Technological University.
6. Leong, C., et al. (2002). NTU book. In *The NTU story, Part II—Coming of age*. Singapore: Nanyang Technological University.
7. External Review Panel, Quality Assurance Framework for Universities, Validation Report on Nanyang Technological University, 2005.
8. Lim, C. P., et al. (2005). *Autonomous universities, towards peaks of excellence*. Report of the Steering Committee to Review University Autonomy, Governance and Funding, 4th April 2005.
9. Massachusetts Institute of Technology Internal Report, *Strategic review of National University of Singapore and Nanyang Technological University engineering curriculum*, 16th June, 1998.

Open Access This chapter is licensed under the terms of the Creative Commons Attribution 4.0 International License (http://creativecommons.org/licenses/by/4.0/), which permits use, sharing, adaptation, distribution and reproduction in any medium or format, as long as you give appropriate credit to the original author(s) and the source, provide a link to the Creative Commons license and indicate if changes were made.

The images or other third party material in this chapter are included in the chapter's Creative Commons license, unless indicated otherwise in a credit line to the material. If material is not included in the chapter's Creative Commons license and your intended use is not permitted by statutory regulation or exceeds the permitted use, you will need to obtain permission directly from the copyright holder.

Making Ideas Work for Society: University Cooperation in Knowledge Transfer

6

Jozef Ritzen

List of abbreviations	
EU	European Union
GDP	Gross domestic product
KT	Knowledge transfer
OECD	Organization for Economic Cooperation and Development
R&D	Research and development
UAE	United Arab Emirates
WEF	World Economic Forum

1 Introduction: KT (Knowledge Transfer) as an Imperative for a University

1.1 It's Ideas That Count for Progress

It was a shock when economists (in the 1950s) realized that economic growth could only partly be accounted for by investments in buildings, machines, and land ("physical capital"). The "wealth of nations" [1] was apparently not only in physical capital as Smith (and with him most economists) had believed for some 200 years. The part of economic growth not explained by physical capital, the "residual," was attributed to ideas and knowledge derived from research and incorporated in people [2]. The 2018 Nobel Prize for economics was awarded to Paul Romer in recognition of his contribution to deepening our understanding of the roles of ideas and well-trained (wo)manpower as drivers of sustainable economic growth [3].

Ideas arise everywhere, but they are more likely to be the result of organized research as happens in universities or other research institutes. The ideas and the new knowledge, however, may easily remain in the confines of the university halls and rooms. Making them work for society is the topic of this chapter, with an emphasis on how university cooperation can contribute in this respect.

1.2 KT as an Imperative for a University

Universities are known to provide education and to do research. Beyond these goals, universities should also pursue, according to their charters, "knowledge transfer" (KT) or "knowledge valorization." Universities can have a substantial impact on the economy of the world, their country, and in particular, their region, through KT. KT is a term used to encompass a broad range of activities to support mutually beneficial collaborations between universities on the one hand and businesses and the public sector on the other hand. These collaborations tend to enhance, first and foremost, the economic growth of the region as most of the benefits of the new knowledge, whether patented or not, contribute most directly to the places where the knowledge is generated.

KT of a university is described as a "contact sport;" "it works best when people meet to exchange ideas, sometimes serendipitously, and spot new opportunities" [4]. Technology transfer is a subcategory: It concerns the transfer of innovative solutions to problems that are protected by different intellectual property rights.

Unlike in education and research, collaborations in KT over long distances are mostly among the top universities in the world. For other universities, the collaborations are mostly in the region or are in the form of "learning from each other's experiences."

1.3 Content of This Chapter

Making ideas work for society: That is the role which universities have in addition to education and research. Section 2 presents the development of the awareness of KT in

---

J. Ritzen (✉)
Maastricht University, Maastricht, The Netherlands
e-mail: j.ritzen@maastrichtuniversity.nl

© The Author(s) 2020
A. Al-Youbi et al. (eds.), *Successful Global Collaborations in Higher Education Institutions*,
https://doi.org/10.1007/978-3-030-25525-1_6

universities and in society at large. These days, most universities around the world have recognized the importance of contributing to society through KT—often with the universities in Silicon Valley as shining examples. The awareness of KT as one of the drivers of innovation has been increasing in the past decades. Innovation itself is increasingly recognized as an important driver of sustainable economic growth. Countries strive to be high up on the international innovation ranking index.

This book is written in the context of King Abdulaziz University in Jeddah, Saudi Arabia. All of the oil-rich countries on the Arabian Peninsula strive toward less economic dependency on oil revenues. In Sect. 2.3, we briefly discuss the role of innovation toward decreased oil dependency.

In Sect. 3, we explore in more detail KT at the level where it happens: the individual university and its impact on the region. In Sect. 4, we consider the crucial factors, which contribute to valorization and how to organize KT in a university. In Sect. 5, we look into existing forms of cooperation, and Sect. 6 presents conclusions.

2 Competitiveness Through Innovation; Innovation for Less Oil Dependency

2.1 Valorization and Innovation

In 1938, one of the first university spin-offs was created by Bill Hewlett, a student of Stanford University, encouraged by his Professor Fred Terman to start a company based on an idea from his own master's thesis. He then founded, together with his colleague David Packard, Hewlett-Packard Company. HP became a huge success: It was ranked 24th in 2004 and 48th in 2018 out of 500 best prospering companies in the USA [5].

HP was the beginning of Silicon Valley: the notion that the proximity between the university knowledge of top universities and business could create high technology agglomerations, with high economic growth as a result. However, being a top university does not automatically imply a high contribution to the region through KT: Several high-quality universities such as Berkeley, Cal Tech, Columbia, Chicago, Harvard, and Johns Hopkins have hardly played a vital role as incubators for the high-tech industry in the region. Varga concludes: "The same university research expenditure was associated with dramatically different levels of innovation" [6].

Learning from success stories about the links between business and universities is high up on the policymaker's wish list. Governments call on university leadership to take up the "third goal" of the university (KT) with the same dedication as the first (education) and second (research) goals.

Continental Europe has had a mixed experience with knowledge transfer. In the postwar period (after 1945), the universities, in particular, the technical universities, were important to regain a competitive edge in production in the electronics sector, in the chemical sector, in car manufacturing, and in mechanical equipment, only to mention examples. However, in the period of the rapid expansion of universities from 1965 onwards, the relations with industry, as well as with the region, became looser. The period of the 1990s presented a turning point. It was felt that the European economies had lost their comparative international strength and that this needed to be mended by increased innovation. Knowledge-driven innovation became a key word.

At that time, the European continent was recognized as having a comparative *advantage in creating* knowledge and a comparative *disadvantage in transferring* it to other sectors and turning it into innovation and growth. Europe has produced and continues to produce a comparatively large amount of basic research (around 30% of the world's scientific publications) with less than 8% of the world's inhabitants. At the same time, it used to be unable to get much industrial innovation and economic growth out of it. This phenomenon was widely known as the "European paradox." The "European paradox" was explained as resulting from "institutional factors" [7] like the lack of communication between scientists about current research, the lack of sharing information ahead of wider publication, and limited networks connecting people in companies, universities, research institutes, and elsewhere. The limited university autonomy in many EU countries is hampering KT [8].

The EU set up the Horizon 2020 program (see Web site Horizon 2020) to promote smart, sustainable, and inclusive growth for EU states through research and innovation. The scale and scope of the Horizon 2020 program expanded the past EU frameworks by funding a wide range of diverse activities along the whole value chain, from basic research all the way to market uptake.

The importance of industry-academia links is evident in the strategies of many universities in countries like Finland, Germany, Ireland, Norway, the Netherlands, and the UK. However, in many EU countries, the challenge to make university ideas work for society has hardly (as yet) been taken on.

Table 1 Metrics for innovation ranking

Six equally weighted metrics were considered and their scores combined to provide an overall score for each country from zero to 100	
1. Research and development: Research and development expenditure as a percentage of GDP	
2. Manufacturing: Manufacturing value-added per capita	
3. High-tech companies: Number of domestically domiciled high-tech public companies—such as aerospace and defense, biotechnology, hardware, software, semiconductors, Internet software and services, and renewable energy companies—as a share of world's total high-tech public companies	
4. Postsecondary education: Number of secondary graduates enrolled in postsecondary institutions as a percentage of cohort; percentage of labor force with tertiary degrees; and annual science and engineering graduates as a percentage of the labor force and as a percentage of total tertiary graduates	
5. Research personnel: Professionals, including Ph.D. students, engaged in R&D per 1 million of the population	
6. Patents: Resident utility patent filings per 1 million of the population and per $1 million of R&D spent; utility patents granted as a percentage of world total	

Source [9]

The success of these strategies can be gauged by the competitiveness of the countries. This is the topic of the following subsection.

2.2 Countries Ranked by Level of Innovation

KT contributes to the competitiveness and the level of innovation of the country. Countries are keen to see themselves high on the ranking of innovation. Rankings on innovation make the headlines in the financial and economic newspapers. The general pattern of rankings of countries is well illustrated with the Bloomberg ranking of countries and sovereigns based on their overall ability to innovate [9]. This ranking identifies the top 50 countries by level of innovation with the metrics presented in Table 1.

Other rankings, like that of the World Economic Forum (WEF), are more sophisticated [10]. In 2018, the top 10 ranked economies over the last four years were: 1. Switzerland 2. Netherlands 3. Sweden 4. United Kingdom 5. Singapore 6. USA 7. Finland 8. Denmark 9. Germany 10. Ireland. Northern Africa and Western Asia with 19 economies show that Israel (11th world wide) and Cyprus (29th) achieved the top two spots in the region for the sixth consecutive year. Third in the region is the United Arab Emirates (38th). It should be noted, however, that the WEF report does not include KT from universities as one of the main drivers of sustainable economic growth.

2.3 Innovation in Resource-Rich Countries

This book is written by authors associated with the King Abdulaziz University, Saudi Arabia: a resource-rich country. Oil-rich countries like those in the Arabian Gulf have almost since their inception strived for innovation as a way to become less dependent on oil, both in terms of GDP, or as a percentage of government revenue or as a percentage of exports. They are, however, generally not high on the list of the most innovative countries, despite these efforts. Albassam [11] documents that these efforts have not been very successful in the period 1970–2015, while at the same time, countries like Norway (oil), Chili (copper), Botswana (diamonds), and even the UAE (oil) have become less dependent on their natural resources.

The road toward less oil dependency is paved by innovation, in which KT from universities is an essential part. Yet, KT still has a long way to go in many of the oil-rich countries in the Arabian Gulf. A higher place on the list of the most innovative countries would be important.

In the next section, we discuss the research findings on the way KT works out for the region in which the knowledge creation takes place.

3 Knowledge and the Region

3.1 The Distributed Impact of Knowledge

The first study to show that investments in new knowledge have by and large local effects is from Jaffe [12].[1] He demonstrated empirically the effects of public research and development (R&D) on innovation in relation to the distance between the spot of origin of the new knowledge and its economic impact. The number of patents was used as an indicator for the production of new knowledge. He shows that public R&D has a strong locational impact: the higher the public R&D in the region, the more patents in that region. This is explained by the "spillovers" of knowledge

---

[1]This section draws on a study of the Central Planning Office (CPB) of the Netherlands [13].

toward that region. His findings have been corroborated by a large number of other studies which looked at Austria, France, Germany, Italy, Spain, Sweden, and the EU as a whole. However, the impact of new university knowledge on the region differs substantially between sectors: It appears to be substantial in sectors like pharmaceuticals and medicine, optics, electronics, and nuclear technology, but less so for chemical products or metal products.

R&D investments not only lead to more patents in the region, but also to more product innovations (patented or unpatented) [14]. That effect is even stronger than on patents. This and other studies confirm the hunch that the application of new knowledge is more likely to happen close to the place where it is originated, simply because of the contacts between the people who invent and those who apply. Of course, this does not exclude the application of new knowledge on a long distance. For example, international firms realize new knowledge through central research institutions or countries with central research facilities in selected areas. The personal factor in generating innovation close to the university is borne out by the larger number of partnerships between firms and universities close to the university [15–17].

In general, one expects smaller firms to benefit more from the proximity of (new) university knowledge. Yet at the same time, larger firms may prefer to locate their research-intensive production or their research laboratories close to a university with a comparative edge in their sector. It is then not surprising that Audretsch and Vivarelli [18] for Italy and Ponds et al. [19] for the Netherlands find that both large and small companies in the region benefit from the presence of a university. Also, Ghinamo [20] finds from an analysis of 44 papers on the impact of the university on the region that these support the existence of a genuine spillover effect of university research on regional innovation. To be sure, the studies quoted above are just examples of a large number all with the same conclusion: The region benefits substantially from KT.

This makes us curious as to the measures used to come to this conclusion of substantial benefits and what the impact is of the universities on the region according to these measures.

3.2 Measuring Impact

Impact is part of the "performance" indicators of KT. The other two are: inputs and outputs. Table 2 gives an overview of these three categories of performance indicators.

The Horizon 2020 program of the EU uses 23 similar performance indicators. They add the leverage of venture funding as well as the relation with KT with *societal challenges* to the performance indicators.

Table 2 Classification of indicators of KT performance

Categories	Indicators
Inputs	**Resources**: R&D expenditure; university's governmental income; non-government donations, grants and contracts; industry sponsorship of university research; scholarships; and number of researchers **Researchers' capabilities**: number of publications, citations, projects, and reports or patents done in the past **Researchers' motivation**: number of previous industry contracts in the department/university; number of strategies concerning industry–university cooperation in the department/university; amount of resources dedicated to support cooperation in department/university; and perception of researcher about the benefits from the cooperation with industry **Firms' absorptive capabilities**: quality certificates (ISO); previous collaboration with academia; membership of some association or research group; number of scientists; and structure of employees by occupation and education **Firms' motivation**: number of previous contracts with universities; involvement with university (e.g., alumni, lecturer); and perception of the firm about the benefits from the cooperation with university
Outputs	Patent applications; patents; license revenues; publications; joint publications; postdoctoral or doctoral positions offered within alliance; joint supervision; master and/or doctoral theses; secondment of researchers; intensity of collaboration; spin-offs; meetings; seminars; and workshops
Impact	GDP per capita; total factor productivity; productivity renewal indicator; number and share of high-growth enterprises; renewal rate of enterprises; share of inward FDI per GDP; knowledge intensity of production; success of spin-off companies; productivity growth; turnover growth, export growth, the increase in exports created by new inventions; net increase of jobs, employment growth; recruitment of graduates; and science citation index

Source [41], p. 20

Table 3 Economic effects of a university

	Example
Employment at the university	Number of jobs at the university and related institutions
Income of the university	State contributions, tuition fees, financial benefits, e.g., from book sales and merchandising
University spending	Purchase of goods and services by the university
Income and spending of university employees	Wages, salaries, and social security costs. Expenditures in shops, on entertainment and culture, and on public transportation
Labor market effects	Delivery of educated labor. Heightened productivity effect
Spin-off business	Companies founded by (former) students and university employees, whether employing academic knowledge and technology
Marketing of knowledge	The sale of knowledge in a variety of forms: from ideas and courses, to patents

Source [26]

3.3 Evidence on the Impact of Universities on the Region

Regional scientists have extensively studied the economic impact of universities in the community [21–24]. The impact of the university on the region goes far beyond KT as Wylie and the contributors to his book show [25]. "Universities can affect the lives of many members of the community via their applied research and aspiration raising activities. They create new knowledge, realize it commercially and fix it locally." Lambooy gives an overview of the different types of economic effects as indicated in Table 3 [26].

Originally, the impact on the region was mostly assessed through employment in the university and the expenditures from students, using regional multipliers [27, 28]. Subsequently, Biggar Economics [29] also included KT activities. The total economic impact of the League of European Research Universities (LERU) with 23 participating universities was computed at 71.2 billion Euros, of which almost one-third was generated by KT (technology licensing, consultancy, contract and collaborative research, spinouts and start-ups, research and science parks, workforce training, and staff volunteering).

In evaluating the role of KT, it turns out that it is often the combination of the supply of well-trained young people and knowledge valorization which makes the difference (see for example [30] for the USA or [31] and [32] for European examples). Knowledge valorization enhances the chances that the graduates of the university remain in the region. This is, of course, relevant in regions with a shrinking and aging population such as Finland [33]. Universities can be important for the investment climate which in turn might seduce firms to locate near to a university.

Grant analyzed 6679 impact case studies of the 2014 Research Excellence Framework (REF) in UK [34] and finds that larger institutions make large contributions to fields such as "Clinical guidance" and "Dentistry," while small institutions make a greater than anticipated contribution to fields

such as "Sports," "Regional innovation and enterprise" and "Arts and culture."

DeVol et al. [35] have made a ranking of the best US universities for technology transfer, with the University of Utah heading the list. The research done at Global University Leaders Forum (GULF) (made up out of the leaders of 27 top universities from 11 countries) is mostly connected to a business in the fields of life sciences and computing. A list of the 20 companies that co-publish the most papers with academics is dominated by major IT firms such as Microsoft, IBM, and Google and by large pharmaceutical companies such as GlaxoSmithKline and Pfizer[2] (see Fig. 1).

Worldwide the WEF has published the ranking of the regions which score highest in international patent filings and scientific publishing. These are listed in Table 4.

Notice the close correspondence between countries by level of innovation and the regions of innovation.

This section brings us to the question of how to organize KT so as to gain the maximum benefits for the region and the country.

4 Organizing Innovation Systems: Making KT Work

4.1 Institutional Setting: Triple Helix

KT does not happen by itself, but requires an institutional setting in which the different actors (knowledge suppliers and knowledge users) find each other easily or are even partners, plus incentives which make the actors move in the right direction. In general, one may say that KT has the best

---

[2]At the background of the strong links between university research and industry in the pharmaceuticals sector may have been the downsizing of the research capacity in the drugs industry in favor of an investment into putting new drugs into clinical trials, while they are looking for smaller biotech firms and universities for the early-stage innovation.

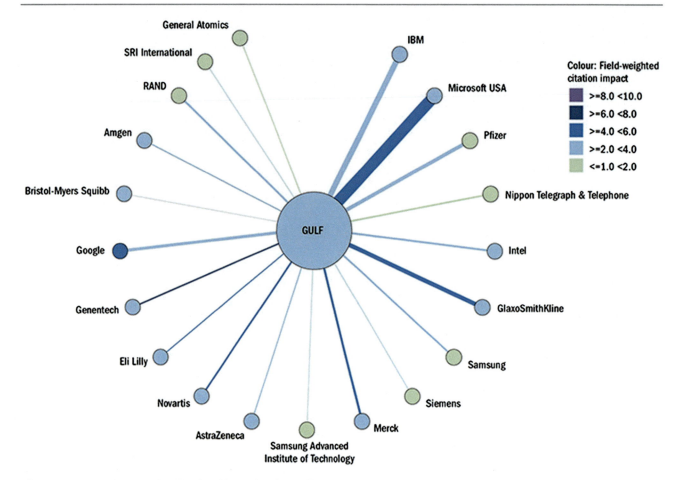

Fig. 1 Connection between GULF universities and industry. **Key**: Node color = institution FWCI (Field-Weighted Citation Impact); Node size = number of publications; Thickness of line = number of co-publications; Color of line = collaboration FWCI. *Source* [42]

chances for success in a compact between the university and the region, often termed the triple helix. This helix has three parties: the local government, the university, and both the public and the private sector [36]. A compact ensures joint strategies. Increasingly universities and regions learn from each other or cooperate in realizing the economic and social benefits from KT from the universities through joint research between universities and industry, start-ups, scale-ups combined with other forms of cooperation (for example, in the education area), as well as with a social commitment of the university toward its setting: the region in which it located. This requires an engagement of the university in incentivizing KT (as we see in Sect. 4.2). But it also needs engagement from the region. This applies not only to the regional government but also to the business community and the public sector in the region. An important element to make cooperation succeed is the availability of angel and venture capital.

Regions with well-developed compacts clearly show substantially more socioeconomic progress compared to regions in which there is little connection between the different partners.

KT goes substantially beyond the patenting of university innovations. Patents can be a source of valorization if they can be applied either by third parties or by university start-ups. But the majority of the valorization comes through new products, improvements in products, or in production technologies which are difficult to patent. The use of new knowledge contributes to a comparative advantage for the first mover. This is also relevant in the context of open science (see Sect. 4.5).

The size of public research is clearly recognized as contributing to innovation. All of the top clusters in innovation in Table 4 receive substantial amounts of public funds [37]. Yet, these funds are often targeted as a result of "industrial policy" toward knowledge creation in the university which is closely related to the business sectors in the region. This underlines that the triple helix not only involves the region. It is best suited for innovation if the national level is included as well.

The institutional framework for KT requires university autonomy in close harmony with the accountability of public universities to their funding agent [8], which is often the public (i.e., the government).

Table 4 Top cluster of economies or cross-border regions within the top 50

1	Tokyo–Yokohama
2	Shenzhen–Hong Kong
3	Seoul
4	San Jose–San Francisco
5	Beijing
9	Paris
15	London
17	Amsterdam–Rotterdam
20	Cologne
22	Tel Aviv–Jerusalem
28	Singapore
29	Eindhoven
30	Moscow
31	Stockholm
33	Melbourne
37	Toronto
38	Madrid
44	Tehran
45	Milan
48	Zurich

Source [10], p. xii

A regional triple helix compact is a good starter for KT, but does require the follow-up of actions at the university level, for universities to be successful in KT.

4.2 Readiness of Universities for Innovation

The EU and the Organization for Economic Cooperation and Development (OECD) have analyzed what it takes for a university to be successful in KT. This happens to resemble closely the insights of Pertuzé et al. [38]. The combined EU/OECD analysis has resulted in a self-assessment tool: HEInnovate [39]. Eight key areas are distinguished for the capacity of the university to contribute to innovation in the region and beyond:

1. Leadership and governance: Strategically, strong governance and good leadership are required for entrepreneurship
2. Organizational capacity: sufficient funding, people, and incentives so institutions can minimize their formal structure which often is adverse to entrepreneurship
3. Entrepreneurial teaching and learning
4. Preparing and supporting student and staff entrepreneurs

5. Acknowledging digital transformation and digital capabilities as key factors for entrepreneurship and innovation
6. Building and sustaining good relationships with a wide range of stakeholders including the public sector, regions, businesses, alumni, and professional bodies
7. Internationalization as essential for entrepreneurship
8. Monitoring and measurement of the size of KT.

The EU and OECD offer to review the engagement of universities in KT through the Regional Innovation Impact Assessment (RI2A). For this review, universities prepare their own case studies which are then assessed by international experts.

4.3 Personal or Institutional KT Partnerships?

Bodas Freitas and others have looked into the quantitative effectiveness of the organization of KT along two lines: personal contractual interactions between academicians and partners outside the university and institutional partnerships [40]. Their econometric estimations suggest that personal contractual interactions are used relatively more by small firms involved in technology and open innovation strategies, while institutional interactions are mostly used by large firms that vertically integrate R&D activities.

4.4 A Practical Example

Here, we present a to-do list for a university which desires to be "entrepreneurial." This is to some extent derived from the practice and good intentions at Maastricht University in the Netherlands.

1. Leadership
   - The university strategy should be embedded in a triple helix. The region should be involved in the development of the university strategy.
   - The university leadership (board and deans) should have ownership for KT as part of their performance agreements. (However, it should be noted that some deans believe that this might be counterproductive.)
   - Goals should be set in terms of the number of start-ups, scale-ups, and other forms of KT which occur within a given time frame.
   - Deans should be rewarded for success in the entrepreneurship of students and graduates and in patenting.
   - Successful entrepreneurs from university incubators should be rewarded with a substantial part of the shares. Clear and trustworthy guidelines should be set up for this.
2. Entrepreneurship Education
   - Research-based teaching (as part of problem-based teaching) should be enlarged to start-up-based teaching: using the examples of start-ups as part of the learning experience.
   - Bachelor and master theses should be devoted to business plans for start-ups.
   - Ph.D. theses should have a compulsory section on "validation," indicating the relevance of the research to society. These validations should be stored in an open access depository which can be consulted by the public and business at large, as a way to "unlock the knowledge safe."
   - A course in entrepreneurship should be included in all disciplines, striving to catch at least 10% of the students. It should be made a compulsory part of the curriculum in economics and business.
   - Alumni who have successfully started companies should be involved in public university lectures or in the regular teaching program. This is one of the ways in which a stimulating environment for entrepreneurship is built.
   - A small number of "entrepreneurs in residence" at the university should be involved in teaching and research in entrepreneurship.
3. Supporting Structures
   - An incubator for start- and scale-ups should be developed. The incubator should be supported with angel and venture capital supplied or organized by the university. New businesses should be supported in the incubator with assistance in marketing and administration.
   - An entrepreneurship center should be created for the delivery of entrepreneurship courses. The center should also lead pre-incubation services with angel funding from the university. Students should be allowed to start a business in the center as part of their credits. The university should own only a small percentage of the shares of the start-up.
   - One or two entrepreneurship weeks should be organized annually to inspire students to become entrepreneurs and to discuss successful practices of start-ups including how to find funding.
   - Master courses in engineering and science should be established on industrial sites related to the master courses, making the research facilities of businesses part of the university campus.
   - The returns of start-ups and spin-offs should accrue mostly to the individuals who have supplied the entrepreneurship.
   - Entrepreneurial achievements and patents should be recognized on par with academic publications for academic careers.
   - A department of the economic analysis of innovation should be set up.
   - Four faculties should take the lead: economics (financial and business services), medicine, science, and engineering.
   - An annual university entrepreneurship prize should be established for the most promising start-up of that year.

4.5 Open Science

At present, there is a substantial drive to do research as "open science", implying that research findings are accessible to the broad public and not locked into intellectual property rights. The main purpose of open research is to spread knowledge and allow that knowledge to be built upon by giving free access to the information so it can flow without restriction.

Open science allows researchers to apply each other's findings without costs and expands access to students to new knowledge. However, it is questionable whether these advantages are sizeable; accept by reducing costs of peer-reviewed publications for the academic community at large if fees to be paid by authors for publishing are less than the present subscription costs of journals.

The impact on entrepreneurship is undecided. On the one hand, intellectual property rights were established to create an incentive for new knowledge. On the other, open science allows for a higher speed of application.

One notices a move toward more open innovation models involving larger multinationals, like the Structural Genomics Consortium. All the results from this research—into the three-dimensional structures of human proteins—are open access. Firms can still see the long-term potential of using the discoveries for later-stage commercial benefit by being close to the new knowledge generated.

In information technology, open innovation and the sharing of discoveries are more established. Firms recognize the benefits that accrue from that dissemination, including more thorough review, consideration and critique, and a broad increase in the scientific, scholarly, and critical knowledge available.

The bottom line is that open science will increasingly get hold of society, definitely when public research is involved. Open science, if anything, facilitates KT.

5 Cooperation in Innovation

Cooperation in KT goes hand in hand with cooperation in research. Existing forms of cooperation are mostly through three channels:

1. **The region**. This is exemplified in Table 4. In terms of size, this is presumably the largest cooperation worldwide in KT/research. The region lends itself well to cooperation in KT as it can be embedded in a triple helix connecting universities, regional administration, and the businesses in the region.
2. **Top universities**. The cooperation in KT of the "Gulf" universities with top universities has been well documented. Figure 2 gives an overview.
   Notice that the kernel of worldwide cooperation between universities and industries is in the USA and the UK. The impact of this inter-group collaboration on research citations is massive: The darker hue of the lines in the network map shows that the field-weighted citation impact of work co-authored by academics from the institutions is consistently high. On the one hand, many companies are often attracted to large institutions with a

wide breadth of excellent research, but on the other hand, companies may also simply choose to work with their nearest higher education institution.
Continental Europe is still not highly visible in this context, despite the EU efforts. This might be the result of a lesser entrepreneurial spirit among academics on the continent, but it may also be due to too little autonomy for the universities [8] and too little infrastructure in terms of incentives within the university (as mentioned in Sect. 4.2).
3. **Other forms of university cooperation**. There are many university networks like LERU in which universities search for joint interests and joint commitments in education, research, and KT. In contrast to the GULF universities, there is little information available on the size of the KT or the research cooperation in these networks. This category of "other" also includes cooperation between universities through mutual Memoranda of Understanding (MOU). To say it blandly: MOUs generally appear to be little more than a license for the university administration to travel and to learn about experiences elsewhere with little translation to the work floor and little actual cooperation in KT.

University cooperation in KT is hard work, carried out by the work floor: the active researchers. Encouraging and incentivizing researchers is generally the best way forward, with the university administration in the roles of encourager and possibly door opener.

6 Conclusions

Sustainable economic growth is more brought about by ideas, knowledge, and human capital than by physical capital, like machines, buildings, or land. Universities are one of the sources of ideas and of human capital. We focus on the third function of universities, next to education and research, and in particular on KT. KT is highly visible in agglomerations like Silicon Valley. Many countries nowadays have strategies to step up KT as a source of sustainable economic growth. Countries strive for a good position in the rankings of countries by innovation. Generally, the countries which are high on the list are also actively pursuing KT strategies for their universities.

Knowledge is recognized to have its strongest potential impact close to the place where it is generated. This makes a university attractive to the region in which it is located as there is a substantial knowledge spillover from the university to the region. The university contributes to sustainable economic growth not only through the expenditures associated with the running of the university, but perhaps more

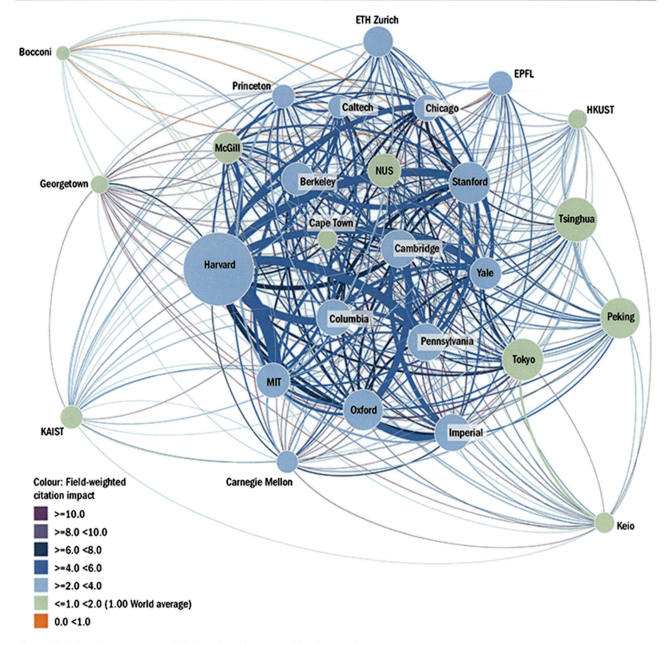

Fig. 2 Collaborations between GULF universities (co-publications university–industry). **Key**: Node color = institution FWCI; Node size = number of publications; Thickness of line = number of co-publications; Color of line = collaboration FWCI. *Source* [42]

by the KT. Smaller firms tend to benefit more from the proximity of university knowledge, while larger firms choose to locate their research close to top universities. KT appears to be substantial in sectors like pharmaceuticals and medicine, optics, electronics, and nuclear technology, but less so for chemical products or metal products.

KT does not come by itself. It requires action and strategy on the part of the university, the region and local public, or private actors (businesses and public organizations). This is captured in the "triple helix" notion: universities, businesses, and regional government should engage in a regional compact which allows for strategies which are closely tuned to each other. National government should also be included. KT is better facilitated if universities have the freedom/autonomy to act without too much red tape. The readiness of universities to engage in KT can be deduced from the commitment of the leadership, from the orientation of the university toward entrepreneurship and from the organizational structure, with attention for an incubator, for the systematic study of innovation and for rewards for success in KT.

Open science (without protecting intellectual property) is increasingly the mode of operation because it increases the speed of KT. Large firms in pharmacy and ICT see the advantages of open science.

It appears that US- and UK-top universities are more prominent not only in realizing cooperation with business, but in cooperating with each other in KT. This is clearly a challenge for universities on the European Continent and for universities elsewhere in the world.

Acknowledgements I gratefully acknowledge comments by Peter Mollgaard, Dean of the School of Business and Economics, Maastricht University and Luc Soete, Former Rector, Maastricht University.

References

1. Smith, A. (1776). *The wealth of nations.*
2. Denison, E. F. (1962). The sources of economic growth in the United States and the alternatives before us. *The Economic Journal, 72*(288), 935–938.
3. Romer, P. (1990). Endogenous technological change. *Journal of Political Economy, 98*(5), 71–102.
4. Minshall, T. (2018). *What is KT?* Cambridge University. https://www.cam.ac.uk/research/news/what-is-knowledge-transfer. Accessed November 1, 2018.
5. Fortune 500. (2018). http://fortune.com/global500/. Accessed March 28, 2019.
6. Varga, A. (1997). Regional economic effects of university research: A survey. *DoNorth.* http://www.donorth.co/appurtenancy/pdfs/varga_effects_%20econ_devel.pdf. Accessed March 28, 2019.
7. European Commission. (2017). *Investing in the European future we want.* Report of the Independent High Level Group on Maximising the Impact of EU Research & Innovation.
8. Hoareau, C., Ritzen, J., & Marconi, G. (2013). Higher education and economic innovation, a comparison of European countries. *IZA Journal of European Labor Studies, 2*(24).
9. Bloomberg. (2015). https://www.bloomberg.com/graphics/2015-innovative-countries/. Accessed March 28, 2019.
10. Cornell University, INSEAD, & The World Intellectual Property Organization. (2018). *The global innovation index 2018, energizing the world with innovation.* https://www.globalinnovationindex.org/gii-2018-report. Accessed March 28, 2019.
11. Albassam, B. A. (2015). Economic diversification in Saudi Arabia: Myth or reality? *Resources Policy, 44,* 112–117.
12. Jaffe, A. B. (1989). Real effects of academic research. *American Economic Review, 79*(5), 957–970.
13. Braam, A. M., Harderman, S., Kiseleva, T., & van Elk, R. (2017, April 4). *De regionale impact van universiteiten; een literatuuroverzicht.* CPB-Achtergronddocument. Den Haag: Centraal Planbureau (in Dutch).
14. Acs, Z. J., Audretsch, D. B., & Feldman, M. P. (1994). R&D spillovers and recipient firm size. *The Review of Economics and Statistics, 76*(2), 336–340.
15. d'Este, P., Guy, F., & Iammarino, S. (2013). Shaping the formation of university–industry research collaborations: What type of proximity does really matter? *Journal of Economic Geography, 13*(4), 537–558.
16. Hong, W., & Su, Y. S. (2013). The Effect of institutional proximity in non-local university–industry collaborations: An analysis based on Chinese patent data. *Research Policy, 42*(2), 454–464.

17. Hülsbeck, M., & Pickavé, E. N. (2014). Regional knowledge production as determinant of high-technology entrepreneurship: Empirical evidence for Germany. *International Entrepreneurship and Management Journal, 10*(1), 121–138.
18. Audretsch, D. B., & Vivarelli, M. (1996). Firms size and R&D spillovers: Evidence from Italy. *Small Business Economics, 8*(3), 249–258.
19. Ponds, R., Van Oort, F., & Frenken, K. (2010). Innovation, spillovers and university–industry collaboration: An extended knowledge production function approach. *Journal of Economic Geography, 10*(2), 231–255.
20. Ghinamo, M. L. (2012). Explaining the variation in the empirical estimates of academic knowledge spillovers. *Journal of Regional Science, 52*(4), 606–634.
21. Maskell, P., & Törnqvist, G. (2003). The role of universities in the learning region. In *Economic geography of higher education.* http://citeseerx.ist.psu.edu/viewdoc/download?doi=10.1.1.456.9141&rep=rep1&type=pdf#page=144. Accessed March 28, 2019.
22. Siegfried, J. J., Sanderson, A. R., & McHenry, P. (2007). The economic impact of colleges and universities. *Economics of Education Review, 26*(5), 546–558.
23. Jaeger, A., & Kopper, J. (2014). Third mission potential in higher education: Measuring the regional focus of different types of HEIs. *Review of Regional Research, 34*(2), 95–118.
24. Goddard, J., & Vallance, P. (2013). *The university and the city.* London: Routledge.
25. Wylie, R. (Ed.). (2018). *Higher education and regional growth; the power of universities to shape local economies.* Policy Network.
26. Lambooy, J. G. (1996). *Knowledge production, organization and agglomeration economies.* Achievement Motivation and Emotion (AME) Research Group, Congress Paper.
27. Garrido-Iserte, R., & Gallo-Rivera, M. T. (2010). The impact of the university upon local economy. *Annals of Regional Science, 44,* 39–67.
28. Kotosz, B., Lukovics, M., Molnár, G., & Zuti, B. (2015). How to measure the local economic impact of universities? Methodological overview. *Regional Statistics, 5*(2), 3–19.
29. Biggar Economics. (2017). *Economic contribution of the LERU universities.* A report to LERU. https://www.leru.org/files/Economic-Contribution-of-the-LERU-Universities-Full-paper.pdf. Accessed March 28, 2019.
30. Winters, J. V. (2011). Why are smart cities growing? Who moves and who stays. *Journal of Regional Science, 51*(2), 253–270.
31. Organization for Economic Cooperation and Development. (2010). *OECD review of higher education in regional and city development: Berlin.* OECD.
32. Organization for Economic Cooperation and Development. (2010). *OECD review of higher education in regional and city development: Rotterdam.* OECD.
33. Haapanen, M., & Tervo, H. (2012). Migration of the highly educated: Evidence from residence spells of university graduates. *Journal of Regional Science, 52*(4), 587–605.
34. Grant, J. (2015). *The nature, scale and beneficiaries of research impact: An initial analysis of Research Excellence Framework (REF) 2014 impact case studies.* Research Report 2015/01. King's College London and Digital Science.
35. DeVol, R., Lee, J., & Ratnatunga, M. (2017). *Concept to commercialization: The best universities for technology transfer.* Santa Monica: Milken Institute.
36. Etzkowitz, H. (1993). Enterprises from science: The origins of science-based regional economic development. *Minerva, 31*(3), 326–360.

37. Mazzucato, M. (2013). *The entrepreneurial state: Debunking public vs. private sector myths*. Anthem Press.
38. Pertuzé, J. A., Calder, E. S., Greitzer, E. M., & Lucas, W. A. (2010). Best practices for industry-university collaboration. *MIT Sloan Management Review, 51*(4), 82–90.
39. European Commission. (2018). OECD. https://heinnovate.eu/en. Accessed March 28, 2019.
40. Freitas, B., Maria, I., Geuna, A., & Rossi, F. (2013). Finding the right partners: Institutional and personal modes of governance of university–industry interactions. *Research Policy, 42*(1), 50–62.
41. Seppo, M., & Lilles, A. (2012). *Indicators measuring university-industry cooperation*. University of Tartu. https://core.ac.uk/download/pdf/25068797.pdf. Accessed March 28, 2019.
42. Baker, S. (2018, January 25). Research that pays: KT at the world's top universities. *Times Higher Education*.

Open Access This chapter is licensed under the terms of the Creative Commons Attribution 4.0 International License (http://creativecommons.org/licenses/by/4.0/), which permits use, sharing, adaptation, distribution and reproduction in any medium or format, as long as you give appropriate credit to the original author(s) and the source, provide a link to the Creative Commons license and indicate if changes were made.

The images or other third party material in this chapter are included in the chapter's Creative Commons license, unless indicated otherwise in a credit line to the material. If material is not included in the chapter's Creative Commons license and your intended use is not permitted by statutory regulation or exceeds the permitted use, you will need to obtain permission directly from the copyright holder.

Student Exchange: The First Step Toward International Collaboration

7

Abdullah Atalar

1 Introduction

In light of globalization in the twenty-first century, businesses are seeking employees with skills that would make them more competitive in the international arena. Hence, the graduates of universities need to have the ability to interact with people from other cultures and different backgrounds [1] to be successful in the international labor market. They are required to work in multicultural teams and speak other languages. This creates new challenges for institutions of higher education [2]. Universities must prepare their students for such a globalized environment, thus enabling their graduates to be more employable. There is a growing pressure on the faculty and administration of universities to internationalize their campuses, curricula and classrooms. They need to prepare their students for global work and global citizenship.[1] Their institutions, programs and courses should be positioned to help globalize the higher education environment and to prepare students for global markets. The Organization of Economic Cooperation and Development (OECD) defines an internationalized curriculum as one which has an "international orientation in context, aimed at preparing students for performing in an international and multicultural context, and designed for domestic students as well as foreign students [4]."

One of the most effective methods of developing an international experience is for students to join a student exchange or study abroad program for a semester or two. Such programs help students be multilingual individuals with intercultural competencies and develop lasting friendships in other countries contributing to world peace [5].

Because of these benefits, universities are trying to expand their student exchange programs and encourage their students to participate in such programs. For example, the European Union is providing financial support to European Universities in 37 countries for student mobility through the Erasmus program [6], enabling student exchange in over 900 partner universities. Moreover, many universities offer second or third language courses to make their graduates multilingual. In some universities, such courses are even a graduation requirement. The recruitment of more international and ethnically diverse students is a priority for universities with a serious internationalization goal. The integration of international students with domestic students helps increase the intercultural experience of all students.

2 Description of Exchange Programs

2.1 Undergraduate Student Exchange Programs

An exchange program allows students from two universities in two different countries to spend a semester or two in the other institution while taking courses. Students from the "home university" become visiting students in the "host university" for a limited time to increase their international exposure. This arrangement is made possible by a student exchange agreement between the two universities. Typically, home universities have a minimum grade point average (GPA) requirement for undergraduate students to be eligible for an exchange program. The students also need to satisfy the minimum requirements of the host university. These requirements can include a minimum GPA or a specified level of proficiency in the host country's language. The number of students in the exchange program hosted by the two universities should be about equal in both directions for a sustainable agreement. If an approximate balance is not satisfied over a period of time, the agreement may come to an end.

---

[1]Global citizens are people with skills in intercultural communication and with awareness and respect for cultural differences and the complex and interdependent nature of the world [3].

A. Atalar (✉)
Bilkent University, Ankara, Turkey
e-mail: aatalar@bilkent.edu.tr

© The Author(s) 2020
A. Al-Youbi et al. (eds.), *Successful Global Collaborations in Higher Education Institutions*,
https://doi.org/10.1007/978-3-030-25525-1_7

Students pay the tuition of their own universities only if such tuition exists. They take courses at the host institution to be counted toward the degree requirements in their home institution. Students bear the costs of travel, accommodation, food and books while they are at the host institution.

2.2 Graduate Student Exchange Programs

To increase research collaboration between two universities, a graduate student exchange program is a useful tool. In such a program, for example, graduate students may spend a period in the host university possibly using the facilities or equipment of the host university not available at the home institution. In the same period, it is also possible for graduate students to take courses in the host university not given in the home university. In a typical arrangement, the host institution provides a tuition waiver and stipends and/or free accommodation to visiting graduate students.

In many developed countries, the number of students studying (STEM) science, technology, engineering and mathematics subjects is decreasing, and it is becoming more and more difficult to find native graduate students [7] despite the efforts to increase their interest [8]. This is not the case in many developing countries. Hence, the STEM workforce in developed nations depends to a large extent on foreign-born mathematicians, scientists and engineers. A graduate student exchange agreement between a developed country and a developing country and the resulting research collaboration are beneficial to both sides: the developing country supplies highly motivated graduate students while the developed country has a rich research infrastructure and distinguished faculty members. Home universities profit from this arrangement in the form of collaborative research papers and the expertise obtained by the graduate students. Research universities in developed nations prefer to use graduate student exchange agreements as a tool to attract and select graduate students for their Ph.D. or post-doctoral programs.

3 Principles for Operating Exchange Programs

3.1 Exchange Program Coordinators

Every department that is involved in an undergraduate student exchange program should appoint a faculty member or a staff member from the department as the exchange coordinator. The duties of an exchange program coordinator can be listed as follows:

- Inform the students in the department about the exchange system and about the partner institutions.
- Keep in constant contact with the exchange program coordinators of the partner universities.
- Inspect the regulations, academic rules and courses of the corresponding departments in partner universities for the purpose of informing the potential exchange students of the department.
- Advise students about the courses they may take while they are in partner universities. Before the students depart for the host country, it is important for students to know how they will satisfy the home institution's requirements with the courses they take at the host university. It is obviously undesirable if the courses taken abroad are not counted toward the degree requirements of the home institution.
- Be a contact point for the outgoing students and be available when they need academic advice.
- Report to the department the grades of the courses taken abroad by the outgoing exchange students upon their return, possibly after converting them using an equivalency table.

3.2 Transfer of Undergraduate and Graduate Credits

There may be differences in the grading policies of different institutions. For this reason, some universities only transfer the number of successfully completed courses in the host institution toward the home institution graduation requirements: the students are exempted from an equal number of courses in their home institution's curricula. However, the grades of the courses taken during the exchange period will not be included in the student's grade point average calculation of the home institution. On the other hand, some institutions may prefer to transfer the courses as well as their grades, using a grade equivalency table. In any case, the students should be aware of the consequences of the exchange system and the grades they get abroad before they go for an exchange.

3.3 Thesis Advisors from Both Institutions

In the case of a graduate student exchange program, two faculty members in the partner universities are appointed as thesis advisors for each exchange student. The research subject that the graduate student undertakes should be within the interest and expertise of both faculty members. Any scientific publication that results from this collaboration is typically authored by the graduate student and the thesis advisors from the two institutions.

4 Advantages and Disadvantages of Exchange Programs

4.1 From the Students' Perspective

Students participating in student exchange programs often enjoy and benefit from the program. Many students feel that the insights developed during the program enable them to feel a deeper interest in the country of exchange, making them more tolerant and adaptable to cultural differences. On the academic side, students can choose from a diversity of courses at the host institution, increasing their preparation for the job market or graduate school.

Attending a student exchange program in a good caliber research university is a tremendous advantage for students having a goal of attending a post-graduate program. The grades they get and their behavior during the exchange period in the host institution give the host institution reliable data points if the same student applies for graduate programs at the host institution after graduation.

On the other hand, financial considerations, administration and cultural difficulties are the highest perceived drawbacks of an exchange program [9]. A majority of students do not apply to an exchange program if there is no financial support. The European Union's Erasmus program tries to alleviate this problem by providing significant financial support for students participating in an exchange program among the universities of the member countries.

Administrative difficulties such as visa requirements, university bureaucracy or difficulty with the equivalency of courses taken may also deter students from joining an exchange program. Countries having difficulty attracting exchange students should spend a significant effort to reduce such problems. The perceived difficulty of the university bureaucracy may be reduced as a result of this effort, helping the domestic students as well. Countries having difficulty attracting exchange students should also consider easing visa and residence permit requirements for exchange students.

Moving to a new country and entering a new culture can be very challenging. Many students may be confused or stymied by the differences they encounter especially during the first month of their visit [10]. Many students end up experiencing some degree of "culture shock." For example, food served may be the most difficult aspect of their experience, contributing to culture shock. This shock could be in the form of feelings of frustration, anxiety or anger, a lack of motivation or a constant sense of being ill. These are all normal reactions when adjusting to a new lifestyle. The adaptation period may not be so easy. Many students feel that going through this difficult time makes them stronger persons in the end. They certainly will have interesting stories to share with family and friends upon their return home.

Evidence shows that many of the exchange programs are within the countries of the developed world. Students prefer to remain in their *comfort zone*, staying away from universities in the developing world, avoiding more challenging and possibly more rewarding experiences. Analyses also show that students who participated in student exchange programs start jobs with higher salaries and have a higher probability of opting for graduate programs [11].

4.2 From the University's Perspective

There is a tendency in many western universities to increase their tuition income through full-time international students [12]. Giving full or partial scholarships to international students and increasing the number of exchange students help increase the number of fee-paying international students. Many universities in the UK, USA and Australia are particularly successful in recruiting international students, capitalizing on the fact that English is the language of the country as well as the medium of instruction in the university. Because of international student fees covering the full cost of the students, revenues from the export of education services have become an important part of the budgets of such universities. Many universities have lifted the quotas that previously limited the number of foreign students.

On the other hand, a significant number of other countries encourage their universities to increase their foreign student counts and exchange student counts, not for the purpose of increasing university revenues, but to cultivate soft power and subsequently increase international trade between the countries. Obviously, this aim can be fulfilled only if international students have a positive experience in the country they visit. In such a case, full-time international or exchange students become natural ambassadors, whether they stay in that country or return to their home countries. They engage in trade and contribute to the relations between the countries in a positive way [13]. This engagement has become so common that in the world university rankings [14, 15], the percentage of international students has become one of the factors contributing to rankings. This factor contributes 2.5–5% toward the overall ranking. It is believed that student mobility is a soft power strategy increasing international trade and the influence of countries on each other. In addition, the experiences of students participating in exchange programs in a university in the developed world may, in the long run, impact political institutions and influence political behavior in their home countries in a positive direction [16].

Many developed nations have difficulty finding good quality students for their Ph.D. programs. Having attractive undergraduate student exchange programs is a powerful tool to attract good quality students to the Ph.D. programs of the host institutions. If the home institution is in a developing nation, outgoing exchange students usually have a better academic standing than the average. It is observed that those students prefer to apply to graduate programs of universities where they spent a semester or two as an exchange student.

Developing nations also try to attract foreign students to their universities to gain prestige and to improve the cultural composition and diversity of the student body. To make their exchange programs attractive for students from developed nations, some universities provide free accommodation for exchange students.

Since English is the dominant language of the world, having English as the medium of instruction makes a host institution very attractive [17]. Students with higher GPA's end up in such institutions as exchange students. If their experience is positive, they prefer to apply for graduate programs in those universities. For example, most of the universities in the Netherlands have English as the medium of instruction, and as a consequence they are very successful in attracting good international undergraduate and graduate students. Although France is the number one tourist destination of the world, the number of international students in French universities lags behind the USA, Britain and Australia. The French government is simplifying student visa regulations and is encouraging its universities to teach more courses in English to lure foreign students [18], and the number of such courses has increased fivefold in the last four years.

5 Maintaining Exchange Programs

5.1 Things to Do

1. **Universities should setup an "international office" that takes care of full-time international students and exchange students**. This office should have the responsibility to recruit such students. It should also provide help and information to incoming exchange students while they are getting their visas or residence permits. If needed, the embassy of the host country in the home country of the student should be contacted to ease the bureaucratic processes. In short, everything related to international and exchange students should be done under the umbrella of this office.

2. **A host family system should be setup for the accommodation of exchange students during their visit**. With such a system, exchange students are more immersed in the culture of the country as compared to a system where the students live in a dormitory. Being a host family is often a voluntary service and there might be no monetary compensation, although some countries may allow a tax deduction for such a voluntary service.

3. **The international office should organize orientation programs for the exchange students during their first week**. During this program, the office should give printed documents, pamphlets or links to web pages which provide useful information to the exchange students in their initial difficult weeks. The information package should include things like the history of the university and information about campus life, entertainment venues, concert halls, museums, local currency, banking, food, cafes, pubs, restaurants, sports facilities, course registration methods, the grading and credit system, the library, computer facilities, traffic rules, shopping, places of worship, bookstores, safety matters, health care, the smoking policy, medical insurance, housing, transportation, parking, useful websites and travel information.

4. **The international office should also organize a welcome picnic in the first week**. This can provide a good start for exchange students and give them a chance to meet each other and local students.

5. **The international office should create a well-maintained website devoted to exchange students**. An e-mail group, a Facebook account or a Twitter account may also serve as a way to distribute information.

6. **The international office should organize cultural trips to nearby destinations**. For example, archeological sites, museums or touristic/historic nearby cities or locations may be good choices.

7. **The international office should inform the students about the academic rules and regulations**. While plagiarism and cheating may be common in some countries [19], such actions may be harshly punishable in some other countries.

8. **The international office should inform the students about the laws of the country**. For example, some countries have strict laws about alcohol or drug use, while in some others the rules on the use of such drugs or substances may be very liberal.

9. **The university should provide local language courses designed for international students**. Such courses must be designed to be useful in day-to-day life with an emphasis on vocabulary and pronunciation components

rather than a fully academic language course with grammar, reading and writing components.

10. **The international office should provide psychological counseling** for those students who are in culture shock or in some kind of difficulty.
11. **The international office should organize regular social events bringing domestic and international students together.** Students who participated in international exchange programs previously may be invited to such events since they are usually more willing to participate in such occasions. It is also very desirable to organize a social good-bye event at the end of the semester for the exchange students leaving for their home countries.

5.2 Things not to Do

The host university should not ignore the special needs of international students. The absence of an international office or an international office not doing its job properly may cause a decrease in the number of incoming exchange students. It should not be overlooked that word of mouth of visiting students is an important aspect of the university's prestige building.

6 Termination of Exchange Programs

6.1 Things that Can Go Wrong

If the balance of incoming and outgoing students is not even, there may be problems in the long run. Many exchange agreements include a clause that enables termination of the agreement if a balance of the number of incoming and outgoing students is not satisfied within a specified time period. Negative political developments and relations between the countries or safety concerns arising from terrorism in countries may also force the home universities to cancel or discourage exchange programs to those countries, reducing the number of incoming exchange students in victim countries.

7 Good Examples of Exchange Programs

7.1 European Union Erasmus Program

The Erasmus [6] exchange program of the European Union was started in the late 1980s. The purpose of the program is to increase cooperation between the partner countries by aiding the growth of international study and giving students an excellent chance to experience another country [20]. Students typically go to another country for three to twelve months. Between 2014 and 2017, each year about 300,000 university students joined this program to study in a partner institution of another country. France and Germany send the highest number of students (about 40,000 each year) to other countries (see Fig. 1), while Spain is the most popular hosting country (about 42,000 students each year) (see Fig. 2).

In Fig. 3, the ratios of outgoing to incoming student counts are given for different European countries for the academic year 2014/2015. English-speaking or warmer climate countries seem to be popular as exchange destinations, while the students in English-speaking countries are not so willing to leave their universities for experience in another country.

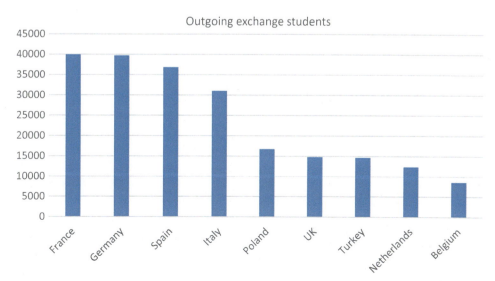

Fig. 1 Number of outgoing Erasmus exchange students from leading countries in 2015 [21]

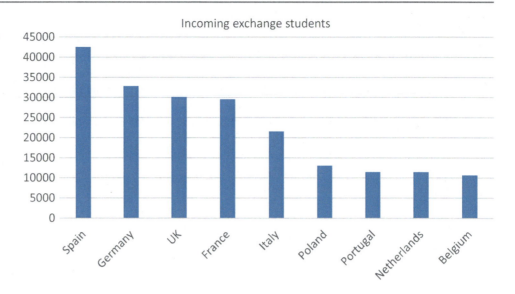

Fig. 2 Number of incoming Erasmus exchange students from leading countries in 2015 [21]

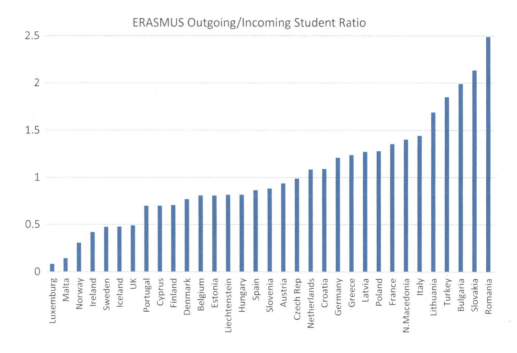

Fig. 3 Outgoing to incoming exchange student ratio for the ERASMUS program of different countries (2015) [21]

In the Erasmus program, students are eligible to receive grants for studying or for being trained abroad for a maximum of 12 months per each of the three cycles of study:

1. Bachelor degree programs
2. Master or equivalent degree programs
3. Doctoral degree programs.

Students registered in a higher education institution in the partner countries and enrolled in a study program leading to a recognized degree or a tertiary level qualification (up to the level of Doctorate) are eligible. The exchange program is carried out through inter-institutional agreements between the receiving and sending institutions. All such institutions must be awarded the Erasmus Charter for Higher Education. In 2015, the European Union contributed about 1500 Euros for each student participating in the exchange program to help cover the extra costs [21].

7.2 Other Examples

AFS-USA is a non-profit organization providing international learning experiences and study abroad programs in 80 countries for the purpose of fostering peace in the world [22]. Most exchange students are high-school graduates, spending one year or one semester in a host institution in another country. A network of volunteer host families worldwide provides accommodation for exchange students lowering the cost and increasing the cultural immersion.

8 International Collaborative Courses, Another Avenue for Student Exchange

Through the advances in communication and Internet technologies, a new type of learning environment is emerging [23]. Digital network technologies have a great potential for Internet-based collaboration, shared knowledge making and joint action across the boundaries of nations [24]. Instead of limiting teaching to local traditional classrooms, this new type of online classroom provides a multilingual and highly diverse learning environment. In such cross-border classrooms, students are required to collaborate with students from overseas for the purpose of solving a problem within the framework of courses they take in their own universities. They face multiple perspectives and multiple approaches in the solution of the problem, making the learning experience more valuable [25]. In a typical setting, the instructors on each side should have prior online meetings to organize the course, possibly by using video conferencing methods. Students are formed into four- to six-member teams with an equal number of students from both sides. A web-based course management system like Moodle [26] detailing goals, lesson plans and assignments is a very useful component of the course. Discussion forums in such course management systems provide a fruitful environment for discussion. Such discussion forums are especially convenient if the collaborating universities lie in quite different time zones.

If the time zones are not so different, possible collaboration technologies among the students of two universities include instant messaging applications like WhatsApp [27] and face-to-face communication and video conferencing applications like Skype [28] or Facetime. Obviously, popular social media tools [29] like Facebook [30] or Twitter [31] can also be used for such courses, making collaboration among students even more interesting. Project reports and presentations can be prepared using cloud-based tools like Google Docs [32] where the students can create and edit the reports or presentations online in a collaborative manner. Such courses not only bring the students of two universities together, but also the instructors from both sides and increase the collaboration and understanding between them. Such relations and partnerships may eventually lead to dual degree programs involving the two universities.

9 Other Forms of Collaboration

9.1 Faculty Exchange Programs

Many research universities have sabbatical programs. Sabbaticals are paid leaves for a period of six months to 12 months for the purpose of professional development [33]. Typically, faculty members are eligible for sabbatical leaves after six or seven years of service. This paid leave period should not be interpreted as an increased vacation period; rather it is an investment of the university to increase the efficiency of the research and teaching force [34]. It also serves the faculty member on sabbatical as relief from routine work duties, providing an opportunity for renewal.

Faculty members who are eligible for a sabbatical program may want to apply to higher caliber universities for a prospect to spend a year. Those host institutions may prefer to accept such applications if the faculty member on sabbatical can teach one course or if the faculty member can contribute to research, without a long-term commitment to that faculty member. Sending institution benefits from the teaching experience gained by the faculty member or from the research collaboration which may have resulted.

In addition, two universities of nearly equal standing may want to sign faculty exchange agreements. Some universities have faculty exchange programs which provide benefits for faculties as well as their universities. An opportunity to lecture in another university is an invaluable experience [35]. Experience abroad helps faculty members enhance their understanding of global issues. Research collaborations can start during the time the faculty member interacts with the host institution's faculty. Upon return to their home institutions, those faculties increase global content in their courses, bringing a clear benefit to their home institutions. Many research collaborations started during a faculty visit continue for many years if both sides find it fruitful. Such collaborations bring the two partner universities even closer [36].

The Erasmus program of the European Union also supports higher education staff mobility between European countries. In 2017, about 62,000 faculty members benefited from this program. Poland sent the highest number to other countries while Spain received the highest number of visitors. Figure 4 depicts the number of faculty exchanged between different countries for the year 2017. In the same year, the Erasmus program of the European Union contributed on average 1872 Euros per staff member to support the short-term mobility.

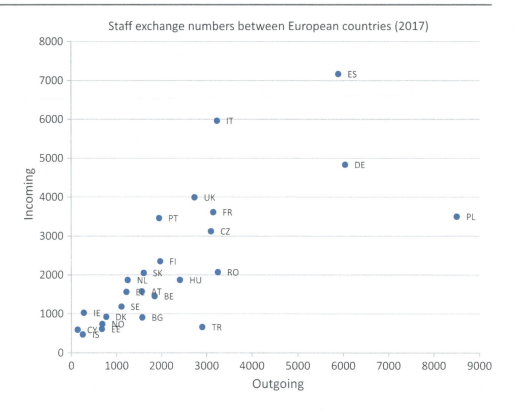

Fig. 4 Faculty exchange counts for European countries supported by the Erasmus program (2017) [21]

9.2 International Joint or Dual Degree Programs

In a typical undergraduate joint or dual degree program, the students spend two years in one institution and two years in another institution. With successful completion of four years in a dual degree program, the students get two separate diplomas from each institution. In the case of a joint degree program, the students receive a single diploma containing the seals and signatures of both universities. In both cases, the students pay the corresponding tuition of the institutions only for the time spent in that institution.

Joint or dual degree master's programs are more widespread. It is believed that joint or dual degree programs better prepare students in terms of academic and intellectual capabilities. Obviously, gaining qualifications from more than one country increases the chance of employment. Graduates of such programs can be more suited to be leaders in international ventures [37]. Typically, students with higher ambitions choose such programs.

9.3 Research Workshops Between Two Institutions

The faculty members from two universities can arrange a research workshop lasting one or two days. This can be considered a mini conference where the faculty members from both sides present their latest findings in their research area. Informal dinners and social events can help faculty members from each side to come closer together. In a typical arrangement, the host institution covers all costs related to accommodation, food and transportation from and to the airport, while the visiting faculty members pay their own airfare. Many European Union research programs sponsor such events to increase collaboration between the member countries. In successful collaborations, regular research workshops are held every year with alternating hosts.

10 Conclusion

Universities in both developing and developed nations use student exchange as the first mechanism to increase collaboration between universities. It is also used to attract full-time international undergraduate students for increased tuition income and to lure graduate students for a stronger research program. The presence of international exchange students in a university improves the diversity in the classroom and the interaction of students with different cultures, developing the intercultural competencies of the students and helping them become global citizens. In the long run, such a program aids trade between the countries and contributes to good relations, to understanding between nations and eventually to world peace.

References

1. Fantini, A. E., Arias-Galicia, F., & Guay, D. (2001). *Globalization and 21st century competencies: Challenges for North American higher education.* http://conahec.org. Accessed September, 2018.
2. Rizvi, F. (2006). Internationalization of curriculum: A critical perspective. In *The SAGE handbook of research in international education* (pp. 337–350). Thousand Oaks: SAGE.
3. Stevens, C. R., & Campbell, P. J. (2006). Collaborating to connect global citizenship, information literacy, and lifelong learning in the global studies classroom. *Reference Services Review, 34*(4), 536–556.
4. Organisation for Economic Co-operation and Development. (1996). *Internationalizing the curriculum in higher education.* Paris: OECD.
5. Clinton, W. J. (2000). *Proclamation international education week.* Washington, DC: The White House.
6. European Union. Erasmus programme. http://www.erasmusprogramme.com. Accessed September, 2018.
7. Hossain, M., & Robinson, M. G. (2012). How to motivate US students to pursue STEM (science, technology, engineering and mathematics) careers. *US-China Education Review A, 4,* 442–451.
8. VanMeter-Adams, A., Frankenfeld, C. L., Bases, J., Espina, V., & Liotta, L. (2014). Students who demonstrate strong talent and interest in STEM are initially attracted to STEM through extracurricular experiences. *CBE-Life Sciences Education, 13,* 687–697.
9. Bakalis, S., & Joiner, T. A. (2004). Participation in tertiary study abroad programs: The role of personality. *International Journal of Education Management, 18*(5), 286–291.
10. Zhou, Y., Jindal-Snape, D., Topping, K., & Todman, J. (2008). Theoretical models of culture shock and adaptation in international students in higher education. *Studies in Higher Education, 33*(1), 63–75.
11. Messer, D., & Wolter, S. C. (2007). Are student exchange programs worth it? *Higher Education, 54*(5), 647–663.
12. Altbach, P. G., & Knight, J. (2007). The internationalization of higher education: Motivations and realities. *Journal of Studies in International Education, 11*(3/4), 290–305.
13. Haugen, H. O. (2011). China's recruitment of African university students: Policy efficacy and unintended outcomes. *Globalisation, Societies and Education, 11*(3), 315–334.
14. Times Higher Education. World university rankings: Times higher education (THE). https://www.timeshighereducation.com/world-university-rankings. Accessed November, 2018.
15. QS world university rankings—Methodology: Top universities. https://www.topuniversities.com/qs-world-university-rankings/methodology. Accessed November, 2018.
16. Atkinson, C. (2010). Does soft power matter? A comparative analysis of student exchange programs 1980–2006. *Foreign Policy Analysis, 6*(1), 1–22.
17. Doiz, A., Lasagabaster, D., & Sierra, J. M. (2013). *English-medium instruction at universities: Global challenges.* Bristol: Multilingual Matters.
18. Campus France: Studying in France. https://www.campusfrance.org/en. Accessed November, 2018.
19. Jones, D. L. (2011). Academic dishonesty: Are more students cheating? *Business Communication Quarterly, 74*(2), 141–150.
20. Gonzales, C. R., Mesanza, R. B., & Mariel, P. (2010). The determinants of international student mobility flows: An empirical study on the Erasmus programme. *Higher Education, 62*(4), 413–430.
21. European Union. (2015). Annex I Erasmus+ programme annual report (Statistical annex). http://ec.europa.eu/programmes/erasmus-plus/about/statistics_en. Accessed February 3, 2019.
22. AFS intercultural programs USA. https://www.afsusa.org/. Accessed November, 2018.
23. Starke-Meyerring, D., & Wilson, M. (2008). *Designing globally networked learning environments.* Rotterdam: Sense Publishers.
24. Kalantzis, M., & Cope, B. (2012). *New learning: Elements of science education.* Champaign, IL: The Learner.
25. Starke-Meyerring, D., & Andrews, D. (2006). Building a shared virtual learning culture: An international classroom partnership. *Business Communication Quarterly, 69*(1), 25–49.
26. Moodle-open source learning platform. https://moodle.org. Accessed November, 2018.
27. WhatsApp. www.whatsApp.com. Accessed November, 2018.
28. Skype: Communication tool for free calls and chat. https://www.skype.com. Accessed November, 2018.
29. Mazer, J. P., Murphy, R. E., & Simonds, C. J. (2006). I'll see you on "Facebook": The effects of computer-mediated teacher self-disclosure on student motivation, affective learning, and classroom climate. *Communication Education, 56*(1), 1–17.
30. Facebook. https://www.facebook.com. Accessed November, 2018.
31. Twitter. It's what's happening. https://twitter.com. Accessed November, 2018.
32. Google docs—Create and edit documents online, for free. https://www.google.com/docs/about. Accessed November, 2018.
33. Davidson, O. B., Eden, D., Westman, M., Cohen-Charash, Y., Hammer, L. B., Kluger, A. N., et al. (2010). Sabbatical leave: Who gains and how much? *Journal of Applied Psychology, 95*(5), 953–964.
34. Kimball, B. (1978). The origin of the Sabbath and its legacy to the modern sabbatical. *Journal of Higher Education, 49*(4), 303–315.
35. Miglietti, C. (2015). Teaching business classes abroad: How international experience benefits faculty, students and institutions. *Journal of Teaching in International Business, 26*(1), 46–55.
36. Sisco, L. A., & Reinhard, K. (2007). Learning to see what's invisible: The value of international faculty exchange. *Business and Professional Communication Quarterly, 70*(3), 356–363.
37. Asgary, N., & Robbert, M. A. (2010). A cost-benefit analysis of an international dual degree programme. *Journal of Higher Education Policy and Management, 32*(3), 317–325.

Open Access This chapter is licensed under the terms of the Creative Commons Attribution 4.0 International License (http://creativecommons.org/licenses/by/4.0/), which permits use, sharing, adaptation, distribution and reproduction in any medium or format, as long as you give appropriate credit to the original author(s) and the source, provide a link to the Creative Commons license and indicate if changes were made.

The images or other third party material in this chapter are included in the chapter's Creative Commons license, unless indicated otherwise in a credit line to the material. If material is not included in the chapter's Creative Commons license and your intended use is not permitted by statutory regulation or exceeds the permitted use, you will need to obtain permission directly from the copyright holder.

Part III

Challenges and Sustainability of Global Partnerships

The Tricky Terrain of Global University Partnerships

8

James Soto Antony and Tara Nicola

1 Introduction

Higher education in the USA, for the most part, is an industry in which individual institutions pride themselves on their autonomy, often behaving as independent actors among a broader population of over 4200 institutions. Even within state systems, which the casual observer would assume enjoy deep coordination among constituent institutions, there is fierce independence and competition.

Take, for example, the University of California (UC) system, which is composed of ten institutions (some widely known campuses include UCLA, UC Berkeley, UC San Diego, and UC San Francisco, for example). One might assume that, because each of these ten campuses belongs to the same state system, there exists considerable cooperation and coordination, even consensus, among the campuses. Yet all ten of these campuses are in regular competition with one another for resources, for the best and brightest faculty and students, and for influence both within the state and across the globe. Where degrees of cooperation and collaboration exist, they do so on the margins in the name of broadly defined system goals that allow all ten campuses to enjoy a set of minimum standards and expectations for policy, for the provision of basic administrative functions (for example, a common application system that the campuses with undergraduate populations use to gather and manage applications), or for overall systemwide priority and direction-setting. But, these ten institutions are, and will always remain, in competition with one another. This is just a cursory description of what happens in one state system. When considering colleges and universities that are truly independent of one another, that are not within the same state system, the competition among these campuses is even fiercer [1–3].

If the model of American higher education, even within what are supposed to be highly coordinated state systems, reflects an attitude of competition and little collaboration, then one might wonder why colleges and universities in the USA increasingly seek collaborations and partnerships with institutions in other nations. Why would the University of Washington actively pursue a partnership with Tsinghua University in China, but find a partnership with MIT, UC Berkeley, or Harvard so challenging to consider, let alone execute? Why would New York University (NYU) desire to open satellite campuses in Abu Dhabi and Shanghai, before opening a campus in Los Angeles, San Francisco, or Seattle? Why would Yale University partner with the National University of Singapore (NUS) to create Yale-NUS, rather than dramatically increase the size of its current campus, or create a second campus on US soil?

We believe the answer to these questions lies in what US-based institutions perceive to be the primary benefits of global partnerships: to increase revenues, to bring about an expansion of institutional reputation and brand, to make the learning of their students and the impact of their scholarship more global, and to gain access to scholarly opportunities not otherwise available. US-based institutions seek to gain a foothold in what they perceive to be emerging markets that contain circumstances that do not exist domestically and that hold promise for dramatically improving their stature and resources. Of course, there are also a host of challenges, and we will discuss these, too.

In this chapter, we will briefly delve into the history of partnerships and collaborations between US-based institutions and global institutions. We will then present a taxonomy that explains the basic types of collaborations and partnerships that exist, describing their elements, what they have in common, and the ways in which they are distinct. After doing so, we will discuss the ways in which US-based institutions that have entered into global collaborations and partnerships have both benefitted from, and been challenged by, these arrangements.

J. S. Antony (✉) · T. Nicola
Harvard University, 13 Appian Way, Cambridge,
MA 02138, USA
e-mail: jantony@ucsd.edu

T. Nicola
e-mail: tara_nicola@gse.harvard.edu

© The Author(s) 2020
A. Al-Youbi et al. (eds.), *Successful Global Collaborations in Higher Education Institutions*,
https://doi.org/10.1007/978-3-030-25525-1_8

Through much of this chapter, we use US-based institutions, and descriptions of their global collaborations and partnerships, as the point of reference. We do this not because we believe that the USA is an exemplar for the world—after all, our extensive global travels as scholars convince us that other nations have much to teach the USA, and that institutions of higher education in the USA would be well served to pay attention to innovations happening in other nations. Rather, we begin our discussion with the USA for two reasons. The first is that many institutions outside of the USA actively seek to enter into partnerships with US-based institutions, especially those with global brand names. So, understanding lessons learned from the experiences of several of these US-global partner arrangements makes sense. Second, the majority of extant international collaborations or partnerships involve a US institution with an institution from another nation.

That said, after situating our discussion within the US example, describing the forms these collaborations and partnerships can take and their associated challenges and benefits, we will widen the discussion with an examination of the broader lessons learned. Specifically, we will discuss the implications of global collaborations and partnerships not just for US-based institutions, but also for those from other nations that might be considering entering into collaborations or partnerships with any other global partner.

2 History of Global Partnerships

The history of global partnerships between higher education institutions can be traced as far back as the seventeenth century. During colonial times, establishing a branch campus to promote the cultural assimilation of settlers was commonplace. The British created colleges in Africa and Australia [4] while the Dutch and French formed schools in Asia [5]. The Roman Catholic Church during this period was also engaged in globalization efforts, encouraged by the Spanish monarchy to establish universities in Latin and South America as well as the Philippines [5]. Colonial powers essentially exported their educational institutions abroad, imposing the institutional model, curriculum, and values of the dominant university in the metropole on the colonial institution [6]. In fact, the export model underlied the foundation of the nine colonial colleges in the US, institutions like Harvard University and the College of William and Mary modeled after their counterparts in Oxford and Cambridge.

During the eighteenth and nineteenth centuries, there was a focus on the expansion and development of US higher education domestically. It was not until the late-1800s that the newly formed US model of higher education, an amalgam of the English liberal arts college and German research

university, was first exported abroad [5]. On account of Protestant missionaries, a number of American institutions were formed overseas. For example, missionaries established the co-educational Christian College of China in 1888 [7], the forerunner to today's Sun Yat-sen University and Lingnan University, as well as the Lebanese American University and the American University of Beirut [8]. These international colleges were not actual partnerships between US universities and those abroad but rather autonomous institutions that embraced a US style of education.

2.1 Internationalization of US Higher Education

US institutions did not formally engage in global partnerships until the early 1900s. The early partnerships were limited in scope, focused on short-term study. The University of Delaware was the first US institution to sponsor a formal study abroad program for undergraduates, establishing a partnership with the Sorbonne in 1923. Initially, proposed by Prof. Raymond W. Kirkbridge at Delaware, a World War I veteran who understood the importance of promoting cross-cultural understanding, the Delaware Foreign Study Plan, as it was called, eventually expanded to include partnerships with institutions in Switzerland and Germany [9].

By 1948, the Junior Year Abroad (JYA) program had sent over 900 students from the University of Delaware and other Northeast colleges to partner institutions abroad [9]. Due to the popularity of Delaware's Foreign Study Plan, Smith College established in 1925 its own JYA programs in Paris, Madrid, and Florence [10]. Paris was a particularly attractive destination for these programs given interest among the French in cultivating a positive relationship with Americans, as well as the country's long-standing interest in disseminating its language and culture beyond its national borders [11].

2.2 US Institutions Abroad: 1900s–Present

Sanguine French–American relations laid the foundation for the first international branch campus. As defined by the Observatory on Borderless Higher Education, an international branch campus can be broadly defined as "an entity that is owned, at least in part, by a foreign education provider; operated in the name of the foreign education provider; and provides access to an entire academic program, substantially on site, leading to a degree awarded by the foreign education provider" [12]. In 1921, the Paris Ateliers of the New York School of Fine and Applied Art was founded as a branch of what is today Parsons the New School of Design. Offering courses in scenography, decorative arts, and costume design [13], the Paris school was established to enrich the learning of American students [8]. The campus remains in operation today as the Paris College of Art, although no longer affiliated with the New School [14].

Despite the success of the Parsons Paris campus, other US institutions were slow to develop overseas footprints. It was not until after World War II that there was growing interest in establishing international partnerships. Nearly, 30 years after the founding of Parsons Paris, the Johns Hopkins University School of Advanced International Studies (SAIS) set up a center in Bologna, Italy. Founded in 1955, SAIS was the first American graduate school located in Europe and remains today a leader in the fields of international relations, economics, and social policy. A number of other institutions subsequently opened branch campuses in the 1970s, Boston University, Webster University, the American Intercontinental University, Alliant International University, and the University of La Verne forming campuses in Belgium, Switzerland, the UK, Mexico, and Greece, respectively [15].

By the 1980s, there was a growing interest among US institutions in exploring other types of international partnerships, including bilateral linkage programs such as joint research laboratories, concurrent and joint degree programs ("twinning" arrangements), and franchising [16]. During this same time, US colleges and universities also started to extend their influence beyond Europe to Asia, specifically Japan. A 1986 initiative spearheaded by the USA–Japan Committee for Promoting Trade Expansion ultimately led 30 US institutions to launch branch campuses in Japan as well as bilateral linkage programs and other educational partnerships with Japanese universities [16].

2.3 Global Partnerships in the Twenty-First Century

It was not until the mid-1990s, however, that there was an explosion in the number of US institutions seeking international partnerships, with over 35 overseas branch campuses opening just between 1995 and 2000. By 2015, an additional 179 campuses were established. During this time, regional education hubs also began to form, or regions specifically designed to house branch campuses from multiple institutions [17]. For example, the United Arab Emirates (UAE) has the Dubai International Academic City with branch campuses of the Rochester Institute of Technology, St. Joseph University, and Michigan State University, among others.

Today, there are approximately 250 international branch campuses across 70 countries, serving over 180,000 students; 77 of those campuses, or nearly a third, are affiliated with US institutions [18]. The majority of US branch campuses are located in Asia and the Middle East. In addition, although

there is no official count of the number of bilateral linkage programs in existence, it is estimated there are hundreds, if not thousands, in operation [19]. Evidence suggests that the number of cross-border higher education partnerships will only continue to grow in the coming years [20].

3 A Taxonomy of Global Partnerships

Global partnerships can take many different forms. Our analysis of the numerous examples of existing partnerships leads us to conclude that, despite these differences, all partnerships can be organized into a taxonomy. This taxonomy, which is depicted in Table 1, captures the levels of resource co-dependence and autonomy the partners exercise or maintain, and also describes the nature of programmatic goals. As can be seen in Table 1, there are notable examples illustrating the final three categories. The first two—one-on-one collaborations, and program or center collaborations—are ubiquitous on every university campus around the world, and do not require specific examples for illustration. Inter-program simultaneous matriculation, though theoretically possible, is rare.

3.1 One-on-One Collaborations and Exchanges

One-on-one collaborations and exchanges are typically informal arrangements between two faculty members located at institutions in different countries. These partnerships may revolve around a particular work product, such as a co-written scholarly piece or coordinated efforts centered on data collection. Sometimes these partnerships might include exchanges where one faculty member visits another's seminars or classes, or even gives a talk and interacts with colleagues and students at the other partner's campus. What might begin informally can, with success over time, lead to slightly more formal arrangements in which the two faculty members begin to co-write grants, invoking their home institutions to think through a structure for the sharing of resources. This kind of evolution might also bring together more colleagues from each partner's home institution or even students. What is important to understand is that the pattern typically begins rather informally—centered upon shared intellectual interests—and, with success over time, begins to crystalize and adopt more formal structures.

It should be noted that, although these kinds of one-on-one collaborations and exchanges typically occur among faculty, examples of students following a similar pattern of initial collaboration and exchange exist. Regardless, success over time often can move these nascent one-on-one collaborations and exchanges toward the next stage: program/center collaborations and concurrent degrees.

Table 1 Partnership taxonomy

Type	Description	Examples
One-on-one collaborations and exchanges	Typically, these are informal arrangements between two faculty members located at institutions in different countries. Student collaboration and exchanges also exist, although they are less common	The list of these kinds of one-on-one arrangements would be exhaustive, because they are arranged mostly through personal connections. Every institution enjoys hundreds
Program or center collaborations and inter-institution simultaneous matriculation	Formal arrangements between academic programs or research centers, these collaborations involve the co-sharing of resources and an effort to articulate mutual goals. They can revolve strictly around bringing scholars together to conduct work or they can support students pursuing degrees concurrently at their home institution and the partner institution. Rules or policies that allow students to simultaneously or concurrently pursue degrees at each institution can be instituted, but each institution retains full authority over their own degree programs	The list of center collaborations is exhaustive, as this practice is ubiquitous. Inter-institution simultaneous matriculation is possible in theory, but rare in practice as these are not formal arrangements (i.e., they require an individual student to reach out to each institution to make this arrangement occur)
Joint or dual degree programs	Joint degree programs allow students to work across the boundaries of two institutions, earning a co-branded singular degree that is conferred by both institutions. Joint programs involve much deeper coordination between the collaborating universities and more complex academic and financial agreements	Appalachian State University—Universidad de las Américas Puebla; National University of Singapore—Sciences Po; University of Arizona—Nisantasi University
Satellite or branch campuses	Universities choose to partner with governments to set up US branches of their own brand abroad. For the most part, universities set up their own campus and maintain virtually all authority over the hiring of faculty, admissions, program design and standards, and the granting of degrees	New York University, Abu Dhabi
Co-branded institutions	Institutions partner with a local institution to develop a co-branded university, combining two academic cultures into one. This is tricky to achieve, and few co-branded institutions exist as a result	Duke Kunshan University; Yale-NUS College

3.2 Program or Center Collaborations and Inter-institution Simultaneous Matriculation

Collaborations or partnerships between academic programs or research centers can revolve strictly around research, bringing scholars together to work on problems of shared interest. They can also bring students together to exchange ideas, take a course together, co-study either virtually or in person, and sometimes even pursue degrees concurrently at their home institution and the partner institution. Often, these kinds of partnerships and collaborations evolve from successful initial one-on-one exchanges. However, sometimes these grow whole-cloth from perceived shared interests absent any initial proof-of-concept experiences.

By definition, these kinds of partnerships and collaborations are more formal, involving a co-sharing of resources and an effort to articulate mutual goals. As a result, there is greater co-dependency. Yet, because these collaborations and partnerships are limited or focused in nature, they rarely force the two home universities to engage in complex financial exchanges. Often, each home institution retains complete fiscal autonomy and merely makes in-kind contributions, such as the provision of space or faculty time.

Theoretically, students might wish to pursue, simultaneously, degrees from different institutions. This should not be confused with intra-institution concurrent degrees, wherein a student at one university pursues two different degree programs (such as a law degree and an MBA, at the same time). Inter-institution simultaneous matriculation is rare. This arrangement would enable a student to pursue two degrees, from two different institutions, simultaneously. It is rare because most institutions have policies that do not allow a student to matriculate in two degree programs at two different institutions. Even if this arrangement is possible, students would not cross-register at the two institutions, and faculty from the two institutions would retain their affiliations with, and be paid by, their home institutions. Basically, to enable simultaneous matriculation, a student would have to take it upon themselves to make the arrangement occur, and each institution would have to institute policies that allow the student to do so. Academic requirements would not be merged or reconciled, and students would need to fulfill the requirements of their home institutions. These kinds of arrangements differ from organized, joint, or dual degree programs (which we will discuss next), wherein institutions have collaborated on combining aspects of their programs, allowing students to earn a separate degree from each of the two institutions while fulfilling all the requirements set by each institution (and, typically, paying separate tuition to each university).

3.3 Joint or Dual Degree Programs

As a further-evolved form of partnerships, joint degree programs are increasingly being developed around the world. These arrangements allow students to work across the boundaries of two institutions, earning a co-branded singular degree that is conferred by both institutions. Unlike concurrent degree programs, joint programs involve much deeper coordination between the collaborating institutions (and their degree-granting authorities) and more complex academic and financial agreements. Faculty commitment of time is still often structured in such a way as to allow each institution to retain oversight, as well as appointment and promotion authority, over their own faculty members— co-appointments of faculty at both institutions are rare but, when they occur, are typically honorific in nature. Compensation for the portion of faculty time dedicated to the joint program is often paid from resources generated by the joint program itself.

Because of the ways in which these joint programs are structured, they blend a higher level of co-dependence with the maintenance of individual institutional autonomy. Faculty adhere to the conventions and expectations (both in terms of promotion and rewards, as well as in terms of academic freedom) of their home institutions. But sometimes the autonomy that institutions and faculty enjoy in these arrangements does not easily transfer over to the students who are enrolled in these programs, and there are examples of issues that students might face, especially with respect to academic freedom and freedom of expression. The inherent blending of academic cultures begins to unveil challenges for both institutions, and, because of this, there is a constant need for negotiation and transparency as the program grows and changes over time. Although most of these programs remain niche program offerings, when these programs work well, they can conceivably set the stage for further collaborations between the home institutions. However, the challenges associated with the merging of academic and administrative cultures make these programs very difficult to start and operate. As a result, many institutions find it is easier to broaden their global brand not by partnering with another university but, rather, with another nation's government (typically via its Ministry of Education, or a similar office) to set up a satellite campus of its own abroad. We discuss this in the next section.

3.4 Global Satellite or Branch Campuses

Because it is so challenging to collaborate with another university, we have seen many US universities choose to partner with governments to set up US branches of their own brand abroad. For the most part, universities set up their own campus and maintain virtually all authority over the hiring of faculty, admissions, and program design and standards. Accreditation typically is subsumed under the umbrella of the institution's original accrediting authority, though there may be regional standards with which the institution must comply as well. Degrees are the domain of the institution and are supposed to be the same quality and status of degree as if the student had matriculated at the home location of the institution.

We have seen the most prominent examples of US institutions setting up campuses in the Middle East, e.g., Carnegie Mellon University, Weill Cornell Medicine, Georgetown University, Northwestern University, and New York University, just to name a few [21]. Several other global universities have begun such arrangements, as well (e.g., Paris-Sorbonne University, Abu Dhabi; the London

Business School, Dubai Center; and the University of Wollongong in Dubai, for example [22–24]).

Many American universities rushed to open up branches in the Gulf Region, attracted by the combination of oil wealth and the area's strong desire for help in creating a higher education infrastructure [25]. Local government efforts to attract global universities to develop campuses that would benefit local students often included some form of subsidy, either to the arriving universities or to the students who would enroll. These governments, in some cases, set aside land for the development of the branch campuses.

But, as we will discuss shortly, the challenges of a fluctuating petrochemical-based economy, the struggle to maintain healthy enrollments when relying solely on local student generation, and the inevitable culture shock American institutions and their faculty experience abroad, have made many of these campuses difficult to operate. As a result, some are on the brink of collapse. Whereas the go-it-alone mentality that serves to extend one's own university brand abroad limits the degree of co-dependence and bolsters institutional autonomy, the attractions of distributing the risk and sharing in the rewards that come with truly co-branded collaborations are increasingly being explored. It is to this we turn to next.

3.5 Co-branded Institutions

We have seen, especially in East Asia, a movement in which US-based institutions partner with a local institution to develop a co-branded university. Some notable examples include Duke Kunshan University, Georgia Tech Tianjin University Shenzhen, Tianjin Julliard School, and Yale-National University Singapore. These projects require the creation of an entirely new infrastructure that combines two academic cultures into one. The proposition is tricky, and few co-branded institutions exist as a result. But the movement is gaining momentum, and we suspect more global universities will attempt such partnerships, particularly in China.

Some of these efforts are focused, bringing together the resources of two global institutions to bear upon a set of specific programs or research priorities, such as Duke Kunshan University [26]. Others, such as the Yale-NUS partnership, are a joint creation of an entirely new campus idea, with the aim of introducing the American definition of the liberal arts concept into that nation's system of higher education [27].

Regardless, the number of co-branded institutions that have successfully launched is much smaller than the list of planned collaborations—many have not gotten farther than concepts on paper. In fact, Chinese regulators have closed more than a fifth of partnerships between local and foreign universities as the Communist party tightens its control over mainland higher education [28, 29]. With this action, China essentially cleared up a backlog, closing down concepts that were merely loose agreements but had little chance of ever materializing as actual partnerships.

Aside from this administrative housekeeping, the long-term viability of those co-branded collaborations that have, in fact, been launched cannot be guaranteed. Part of this has to do with the fact that setting up these collaborations, especially in China, requires a nuanced and deeply sophisticated understanding and appreciation of how to do business in the foreign country. Partnering with a Chinese public university amounts to the same thing as doing business with the Chinese government which, essentially, means doing business with the Communist party itself [30]. One must understand party politics and priorities and have deep connections within the power structure of the party apparatus to effectively work with Chinese institutions.

For non-Chinese universities, getting started in China requires a great deal of preparation, cultural knowledge, and a bevy of consultants and partners with ties to the party. These requirements, alone, are not insurmountable. What can make working in China (and, frankly, even within any other part of the world) challenging is when a partner university fails to remember that, when all is said and done, the imperative for the host nation will always be to address its self-defined regional and national priorities. Any global partner that seeks to develop a co-branded institution must not come to the table solely wishing to pursue its own agenda.

4 Benefits of Global Partnerships

Given the high costs, complexity, and amount of time needed to establish these types of transnational partnerships, why are US institutions so eager to form them? Their motivations can generally be boiled down to four key reasons: increasing revenues, expanding institutional reputation and brand, globalizing student learning and the impact of scholarship, and expanding access to scholarly opportunities. As depicted in Table 2, however, some motivations are stronger than others for particular types of partnerships. These four factors are detailed further below.

4.1 Increasing Revenues

Financial considerations are perhaps the largest driving force behind US institutions seeking partnerships abroad. In recent years, US colleges and universities have witnessed drastic declines in government funding, state support decreasing 40% between 1980 and 2011 [31]. Because state

Table 2 Benefits of international partnerships, by type

International partnerships	Increasing revenue	Expanding brand	Globalizing learning	Accessing scholarly opportunities
One-on-one collaboration	Low	Low	Low	Medium
Center collaborations and inter-institution simultaneous matriculation	Low	Medium	Medium	High
Joint or dual degree programs	Medium	High	High	High
Satellite or branch campuses	High	High	High	High
Co-branded institutions	High	High	High	High

appropriations have historically represented a large percentage of the annual operating budgets at public institutions, these colleges and universities have become increasingly cash-strapped and thus eager to explore new funding avenues [32].

For institutions seeking to generate significant revenue from global partnerships, branch campuses and co-branded institutions are the most lucrative options on account of the tuition money they generate. In fact, the University of Arizona noted that a primary reason for opening its 25 "microcampuses" across Asia, the Middle East, and Mexico was the potential revenue raised from student tuition [33]. While some joint degree programs may also increase institutional revenues, one-on-one collaborations and concurrent degree programs are not designed to do so.

Beyond tuition dollars, financial incentives offered directly by host countries are also a major pull factor to engage in these global partnerships, particularly for institutions seeking to establish a branch campus or co-branded university. A 2012 report found that 30% of branch campuses received some type of financial support from the host country. Support can take the form of tax breaks, rent-free facilities, or discounted leases on land [34]. For example, the UAE gifted New York University $50 million in 2013 to establish its branch campus in Abu Dhabi [35].

4.2 Expanding Institutional Brand and Reputation

Internationalization is also a means of strengthening and expanding an institution's brand and overall prestige. US colleges and universities increasingly consider being "world class" as key to their survival in a competitive and interconnected higher education marketplace [2]. This expansion of brand and reputation is a strong motivating factor for establishing joint degree programs, branch campuses, and co-branded universities specifically. This motivation is especially reflected in the marketing materials for such partnerships. For example, Yale-NUS notes that the

co-branded college is designed to "educate citizens of the world," aiming "to spur innovation in higher education across the globe" [36]. Similarly, NYU Abu Dhabi has declared itself the "World's Honor College" [37]. These international programs not only generate positive publicity for the US institutions but also are a marker of prestige [38, 39].

In addition, global partnerships enable US institutions to achieve their reputational goals as well as better carry out their missions. For example, Berklee College of Music was drawn to form a branch campus in Valencia, Spain due to the city's strong music history and traditions, bolstering the college's resources for studying flamenco music in particular [40].

4.3 Globalizing Learning and Impact

Another commonly cited reason for establishing transnational education partnerships is the potential to expand the learning of students as well as the impact of faculty research. Overseas branch campuses enable US students to more easily study abroad and also support the dissemination of faculty research outside the US context [41]. Likewise, bilateral linkage programs and co-branded institutions can spur development of new curriculum or degree programs that incorporate scholarship and pedagogical techniques from the host country [42]. Connections between US faculty and their counterparts abroad can also inspire curricular and teaching development [43].

Perhaps even more important is that international partnerships assist US institutions in recruiting top students and faculty [44]. For example, one of the motivations for Duke University to open Duke Kunshan University (DKU) was to increase the diversity of its student body as well as its faculty. In 2014, only 8% of undergraduates and 23% of the graduate student population at Duke identified as international [45]. Through the establishment of DKU, Duke has been able to attract more students, as well as faculty members, from overseas.

Table 3 Challenges of international partnerships, by type

International Partnerships	Risk to brand	Revenue and enrollment expectations	Control over quality	Threats to autonomy
One-on-one collaboration	Low	Low	High	Low
Center collaborations and inter-institution simultaneous matriculation	Medium	Medium	Medium	Medium
Joint or dual degree programs	Medium	Medium	Medium	High
Satellite or branch campuses	High	High	High	High
Co-branded institutions	High	High	Medium	High

4.4 Accessing Scholarly Opportunities

Finally, all types of international partnerships bolster the research of US faculty through the collaboration and funding opportunities they offer. The Singapore-MIT Alliance (SMA) is one example of a transnational partnership that has strengthened the research capabilities and scholarly development of US-based faculty. Established in 1997, SMA was a research enterprise between the Massachusetts Institute of Technology, the National University of Singapore (NUS), and the Nanyang Technology University (NTU) focused on engineering and the life sciences. SMA supported interdisciplinary curriculum development and research within MIT, led to the publication of hundreds of journal articles by MIT and Singaporean researchers, and provided over $30 million in research money to MIT faculty [46]. Today, the venture still exists in the form of the Singapore-MIT Alliance for Research and Technology (SMART), a collaboration between MIT and the National Research Foundation of Singapore.

The Tsinghua-Berkeley Shenzhen Institute, a partnership between Tsinghua University in China and UC Berkeley, is another example of a successful research alliance. The venture was entirely financed by the Shenzhen municipal government and the Tsinghua Education Foundation, the former contributing $52 million toward the creation of buildings and laboratories and the latter investing $22 million to support student scholarships as well as faculty research in a range of areas including information technology and pharmaceuticals [46]. These international collaborations in many cases can open doors to funding and research opportunities that are otherwise not available domestically.

5 Challenges of Global Partnerships

Our analysis of recent articles written about existing global partnerships suggests that there are four major challenges that are raised consistently. These include: risk aversion and its impact on innovation; lower than expected enrollments and revenue; the perceived erosion of, or lack of control

over, quality; and threats to autonomy and academic freedom. We will discuss each below. Table 3 summarizes the challenges—risk to brand, risk to revenue/enrollment, threats to quality, and threats to autonomy and academic freedom—presented by each of the types of partnerships.

5.1 Risk Aversion and Its Impact on Innovation

Both institutions or parties in any global collaboration must think about the impact the partnership, even if informal in nature, has on their individual brands. Typically, partnerships are in part driven by the promise that it will augment each party's individual brand globally. Though this makes sense from a market-oriented perspective, institutions tend to be risk-averse, only partnering with other institutions that they perceive to be on equal status (or, better yet, even higher status) than themselves. As a result, institutions that initially lack cachet are rarely sought as partners; more often than not, this prevents institutions from seeking potentially high impact partners whose work is transformational, despite their lesser known brand. Places like Harvard University receive hundreds of requests for partnerships, even when those partnerships make little sense. Sadly, another lesser known university might be a much better match for a potential partnership, which could truly be innovative in nature. This phenomenon also impacts higher education's collective capacity to improve opportunity in developing nations. For example, outside of medicine, collaboration between elite research-based institutions and poor nations is lacking [47]. Risk aversion and the protection of (and related desire to improve, by association) institutional brand slow down innovation and out-of-the-box thinking in the global partnership space.

5.2 Lower Than Expected Enrollment and Revenue

Among the many partnerships that have begun, the reality of lower than forecasted enrollments and reductions in spending on research by host governments pushes these collaborations to the brink of failure. For example, there exist many once-heralded collaborations in the Middle East that are on the precipice of bankruptcy. This has to do, in part, with the economy in this region being so volatile because of its lack of diversification (in a petrochemical-based economy, the fluctuating price of oil puts a dent in consumer and government spending). This volatility directly impacts local students' willingness to enroll, as government subsidies can decrease. For many US-based institutions that set up shop in the Middle East, reliance on local or regional student enrollment has put their operations at risk. Only those institutions (NYU Abu Dhabi, as one example) that have branded their Middle East campuses as enrollment options for students from any part of the world seem to be doing somewhat better. The challenge of enrollment and research support maintenance, minimally speaking, is not insignificant. Growing enrollments and research investments remains an even greater challenge.

5.3 Perceived Erosion, Lack of Control Over Quality

Once a partnership is cemented, the question of who controls quality is always evolving. Depending on how the partnership is structured, it can sometimes be difficult to determine who should define academic standards for a program, oversee the hiring and evaluation of faculty, and establish the articulation and assessment of learning goals for students. Local accreditation authorities might have different standards than what the other partner finds familiar, and these different standards may have little to do with academics and everything to do with local imperatives and national economic goals—both of which are subject to shifting political priorities. The challenges here are characterized by a perceived lack of control [48]. That is, the two partner institutions may have little control over the institutionally specific and nationally specific vagaries of policy and politics, all of which invariably bleed over into the higher education space. Sometimes, partners from one national context perceive the other national context to be invested in items associated with efficiency and scale, rather than rigor and quality. The time and energy required to negotiate this landscape can exhaust faculty, leading to lower levels of commitment—a threat to any partnership's survival.

5.4 Threats to Autonomy and Academic Freedom

One of the most commonly cited challenges among global partnerships has to do with negotiating different definitions of autonomy and academic freedom. In the US context, both are prized by academics. Institutions enjoy a great deal of autonomy, especially from obtrusive government interference. And individual academics enjoy, in principle, academic freedom. Both of these can be hard to come by in national contexts where, culturally, conceptions of who controls the academic enterprise, and what constitutes acceptable faculty work, are differently understood. US-based faculty working abroad find that they cannot teach as they would in the USA, at least not without a great deal of scrutiny. Government policies as well as disagreements over hot political issues or curricula that run against the grain of local sensibilities and cultural norms [49] can strain expatriate faculty teaching or conducting research abroad, making daily life uncomfortable and, sometimes, even unbearable. When a faculty member lacks the basic freedoms to engage in their work the way they would take for granted in their home nation, the global partnership risks losing the best faculty. No amount of monetary incentives (many of these arrangements make allowances for higher pay, subsidized housing, and so forth) can ever make up for faculty who feel disenfranchised. Collaborations that fail to tackle, and carefully manage, the issues of autonomy and academic freedom are at risk of long-term failure.

6 Implications and Recommendations

Global partnerships can be exciting, new ventures that yield innovative programs and research for both partner institutions. But any institution that desires a collaboration with another global partner should balance the benefits with a careful analysis, and detailed plan, to address the inevitable challenges that will arise.

As we suggest in this chapter, global partnerships can take many forms—we have illuminated five, in order of increasing co-dependence and shared autonomy. We recommend that institutions, in the beginning, identify and engage in lower-commitment (what we call "proof-of-concept") partnerships, carefully addressing issues that arise and documenting successes. Because so much of the success of partnerships hinges upon trusting relationships, these proof-of-concept arrangements not only serve to build the necessary person-to-person networks needed to manage more complex collaborations, but also stimulate the kind of innovative thinking that yields more ambitious collaborations down the road. In the end, the best partnerships emerge from solid person-to-person relationships that have been forged through working together, managing complexities, and developing a sense of mutual interest and destiny.

We also recommend that any potential global partners take seriously the cultural differences inherent in bringing two institutions from different nations together. Careful negotiation of autonomy, quality determinations, accreditation, academic freedom, and assessment or evaluation of outcomes should occur prior to any formal agreements. These issues should not be ignored—hoping they will manage themselves in situ is a fool's errand. We recommend that potential partners have concrete conversations that lead to the clear identification of potential areas of conflict, and a mutually agreeable method for addressing conflicts when they arise. We also recommend that the parameters for faculty work are clearly articulated, and that expatriate faculty members are given clear descriptions of these parameters so they know what to expect.

We recommend that global partnerships deal with money and resources upfront, and in the most transparent fashion possible. These partnerships should carefully forecast revenues and expenditures and stipulate how shortfalls will be managed (as well as attribute responsibilities for any shortfalls say, for example, if government priorities and investment suddenly shift). The development and ongoing management of the physical plant and any cost-sharing agreements should also be agreed upon in advance.

Relatedly, there should be clear agreements regarding the use of brand, name, and trademark, as well as the ownership of any and all intellectual property. Indeed, branding is not a trivial issue, and global partners should carefully consider how a student graduating from a collaborative program will present their credentials. Partnering institutions should think through, carefully, the implications of branding for any concurrent or joint degree programs. And co-branded institutions should consider what they can do to ensure the value of their degrees rises, in the mind of its graduates and the market overall, to the level the degrees offered by the constituent partner institutions.

Finally, we recommend that any potential partnership be driven by values that exceed the mere desire to raise institutional profile, or to increase revenues and market share. Impact matters, and we believe that the collaborations that will stand the test of time, though heeding the importance of revenue generation, are driven by the desire to be truly innovative and to engage real-world challenges. We believe the opportunity to do great work, in the name both of increasing educational access and opportunity and advancing research, exist in regions of the world that have largely been ignored by elite institutions. We also believe that partnerships between institutions that are not among the typical elite can, and will, thrive in the future as these are institutions that are less risk-averse (at least when it comes to protecting brand), and are more open to try new and innovative ventures.

Mostly, we are eager to remind institutions, in their quest to go global, to resist the impulse to think only of their own priorities and immediate needs. Partnerships that are built upon a foundation of shared interests and mutual respect and are also transparent and egalitarian in their decision-making processes will be those that not only stand the test of time, but also have the greatest positive impact.

References

1. Haynie, D. (2018, January 23). The great game for international students. *U.S. News & World Report.* https://www.usnews.com/news/best-countries/articles/2018-01-23/competition-for-international-students-increases-among-countries. Accessed December 17, 2018.
2. Stanfield, D. A. (2014). *International branch campuses: Motivation, strategy, structure* (Ph.D. dissertation). Boston College.
3. Leland, D., & Moore, J. (2007, September/October). Strategic. *Public Purpose.* http://www.aascu.org/uploadedFiles/AASCU/Content/Root/MediaAndPublications/PublicPurposeMagazines/Issue/sep-oct07strategic.pdf. Accessed December 17, 2018.
4. Pietsch, T. (2017). The 1880s: Global connections and the British settler universities. In A. R. Nelson & N. M. Strohl (Eds.), *Universities 2030: Learning from past to anticipate the future* (pp. 12–14). Leeds, UK: Worldwide Universities Network.
5. Altbach, P. G. (2004). Globalization and the university: Myths and realities in an unequal world. *Tertiary Education and Management,* *10*(1), 3–25. https://doi.org/10.1080/13583883.2004.9967114.
6. Ashby, E. (1964). *Universities: British, Indian, Africa.* Cambridge, MA: Harvard University Press.
7. Wang, D. (2007). *Managing god's higher learning: US-China cultural encounter and Canton Christian College (Lingnan University), 1888–1952.* Lanham, MD: Lexington Books.
8. Lanford, M., & Tierney, W. G. (2016). The international branch campus: Cloistered community or agent of social change? In C. S. Collins, M. N. Lee, J. N. Hawkins, & D. E. Neubauer (Eds.), *The Palgrave handbook of Asia Pacific higher education* (pp. 157–172). New York: Palgrave Macmillan.
9. Contreras, E., Jr. (2015). Beyond the grand tour: Re-thinking the education abroad narrative for US higher education in the 1920s. *International Journal of Tourism Anthropology, 4*(3), 238–251. https://doi.org/10.1504/IJTA.2015.071931.
10. Comp, D. (2016). A historical overview of international education scholarship and the role of the scholar-practitioner. In B. Streitwieser & A. C. Ogden (Eds.), *International higher education's scholar-practitioners: Bridging research and practice* (pp. 73–92). Oxford: Symposium Books Ltd.
11. Walton, W. (2005). Internationalism and the junior year abroad: American students in France in the 1920s and 1930s. *Diplomatic History, 29*(2), 255–278. https://doi.org/10.1111/j.1467-7709.2005.00473.x.
12. Healy, N. (2014). When is an international branch campus? *International Higher Education, 78*(1), 22–23. https://doi.org/10.6017/ihe.2014.78.5808.
13. The New School, About Parsons Paris—History. https://www.newschool.edu/parsons-paris/history/. Accessed December 17, 2018.
14. Guttenplan, D. D. (2012, November 11). Parsons to re-open campus in Paris. *New York Times.* https://www.nytimes.com/2012/11/12/world/europe/12iht-educside12.html. Accessed December 17, 2018.

15. Becker, R. (2009). *International branch campuses: Markets and strategies*. London: The Observatory on Borderless Higher Education.
16. Chambers, G., & Cummings, W. (1990). *Profiting from education: Japan-United States international educational ventures in the 1980s*. New York: Institute of International Education.
17. Knight, J. (2011). Education hubs: A fad, a brand, an innovation. *Journal of Studies in International Education, 15*(3), 221–240. https://doi.org/10.1177/1028315311398046.
18. Garrett, R., Kinser, K., Lane, J. E., & Merola, R. (2016). *International branch campuses—Trends and developments 2016*. Surrey, UK: OBHE & C-BERT.
19. Altbach, P. G. (2007). Twinning and branch campuses: The professorial obstacle. *International Higher Education, 48*(1), 2–3. https://ejournals.bc.edu/ojs/index.php/ihe/article/view/7976/7127.
20. Crist, J. T. (2017). U.S. universities and international branch campuses. *IEM Spotlight Newsletter, 14*(1). https://www.nafsa.org/Professional_Resources/Browse_by_Interest/International_Students_and_Scholars/Network_Resources/International_Enrollment_Management/U_S__Universities_and_International_Branch_Campuses/.
21. New York University Abu Dhabi. Vision and mission. https://nyuad.nyu.edu/en/about/nyuad-at-a-glance/vision-and-mission.html. Accessed February 15, 2019.
22. Paris-Sorbonne University Abu Dhabi. About us. https://www.sorbonne.ae/about-us/. Accessed February 15, 2019.
23. London Business School Dubai Center, Dubai. https://www.london.edu/about/location/dubai. Accessed February 15, 2019.
24. University of Wollongong in Dubai. Overview. https://www.uowdubai.ac.ae/about-uowd/overview. Accessed February 15, 2019.
25. Lewin, T. (2009, December 27). University branches in Dubai are struggling. *New York Times*. https://www.nytimes.com/2009/12/28/education/28dubai.html. Accessed December 17, 2018.
26. Redden, E. (2018, April 4). An Ivy degree, with an Irish twist. *Inside Higher Education*. https://www.insidehighered.com/news/2018/04/04/columbia-trinity-college-dublin-start-new-dual-ba-program. Accessed December 17, 2018.
27. Prihar, A., & Cho, S. (2018, November 8). Yale, Yale-NUS look to strengthen partnership. *Yale Daily News*. https://yaledailynews.com/blog/2018/11/08/yale-yale-nus-look-to-strengthen-partnership/. Accessed December 17, 2018.
28. Feng, E. (2018, July 17). China closes a fifth of foreign university partnerships. *Financial Times*. https://www.ft.com/content/794b77e8-8976-11e8-bf9e-8771d5404543. Accessed December 17, 2018.
29. Redden, E. (2018, July 11). Closures of China-foreign programs. *Inside Higher Education*. https://www.insidehighered.com/news/2018/07/11/chinas-ministry-education-approves-termination-more-200-chinese-foreign-cooperative. Accessed December 17, 2018.
30. Kirby, W. C. (2014). The Chinese century? The challenges of higher education. *Daedalus, 143*(2), 145–156. https://doi.org/10.1162/DAED_a_00279.
31. Mortenson, T. (2012, Winter). State funding: A race to the bottom. *American Council on Education*. https://www.acenet.edu/the-presidency/columns-and-features/Pages/state-funding-a-race-to-the-bottom.aspx. Accessed December 17, 2018.
32. Mitchell, M., Leachman, M., & Masterson, K. (2017, August 27). A lost decade in higher education funding. *Center on Budget and Policy Priorities*. https://www.cbpp.org/research/state-budget-and-tax/a-lost-decade-in-higher-education-funding. Accessed December 17, 2018.
33. Redden, E. (2017, May 23). Going big into 'microcampuses.' *Inside Higher Education*. https://www.insidehighered.com/news/2017/05/23/arizona-embarks-plan-develop-25-global-microcampuses. Accessed December 17, 2018.
34. Varghese, N. V. (2017). Globalization and cross-border mobility in higher education. In T. R. Dash & M. Behera (Eds.), *Educational access and excellence* (pp. 9–24). New Delhi: Allied Publishers Pvt. Ltd.
35. Redden, E. (2013, March 11). Global ambitions. *Inside Higher Education*. https://www.insidehighered.com/news/2013/03/11/nyu-establishes-campuses-and-sites-around-globe. Accessed December 17, 2018.
36. Yale-NUS College. Vision and mission. https://www.yale-nus.edu.sg/about/vision-and-mission/. Accessed December 17, 2018.
37. Redden, E. (2010, June 21). The world's honors college? *Inside Higher Education*. https://www.insidehighered.com/news/2010/06/21/worlds-honors-college. Accessed December 17, 2018.
38. Slaughter, S., & Leslie, L. L. (1997). *Academic capitalism: Politics, policies, and the entrepreneurial university*. Baltimore: Johns Hopkins University Press.
39. Verbik, L., & Merkley, C. (2006). *The international branch campus: Models and trends*. London: The Observatory on Borderless Higher Education.
40. Fuchs, D. (2012, September 17). Berklee College of music opens campus in Spain. *Boston Globe*. https://www.bostonglobe.com/arts/music/2012/09/17/berklee-college-music-opens-new-valencia-campus/ptE7agZxA7EuVZzyjDrZvN/story.html. Accessed December 17, 2018.
41. Lane, J. E., & Kinser, K. (2011). Reconsidering privatization in cross-border engagements: The sometimes public nature of private activity. *Higher Education Policy, 24*(2), 255–273. https://doi.org/10.1057/hep.2011.2.
42. Shams, F., & Huisman, J. (2012). Managing offshore branch campuses: An analytical framework for institutional strategies. *Journal of Studies in International Education, 16*(2), 106–127. https://doi.org/10.1177/1028315311413470.
43. Clifford, M. (2015). *Assessing the feasibility of international branch campuses: Factors universities consider when establishing campuses abroad* (Ph.D. dissertation). Pardee RAND Graduate School.
44. Edelstein, R. J., & Douglass, J. A. (2012). *Comprehending the international initiatives of universities: A taxonomy of modes of engagement and institutional logics*. Research & Occasional Paper Series: CSHE.19.12. Berkeley, CA: UC Berkeley.
45. Huang, C. (2014, October 15). Duke Kunshan University—A bold innovation. *Sanford Journal of Public Policy*. https://webcache.googleusercontent.com/search?q=cache:E0ncwQN7GBMJ:https://sites.duke.edu/sjpp/2014/duke-kunshan-university-a-bold-innovation/+&cd=6&hl=en&ct=clnk&gl=us. Accessed December 17, 2018.
46. Youtie, J., Li, Y., Rogers, J., & Shapira, P. (2017). Institutionalization of international university research ventures. *Research Policy, 46*(9), 1692–1705. https://doi.org/10.1016/j.respol.2017.08.006.
47. Baker, S. (2018, September 21). Ignoring developing countries. *Inside Higher Education*. https://www.insidehighered.com/news/

2018/09/21/study-finds-limited-collaboration-between-research-elites-and-developing-nations. Accessed December 17, 2018.

48. Lane, J. E. (2011). Global expansion of international branch campuses: Managerial and leadership challenges. *New Directions for Higher Education, 2011*(155), 5–17. https://doi.org/10.1002/he.440.

49. Redden, E. (2018, October 29). Cutting ties: Cornell university ends a partnership with Renmin University of China, citing academic freedom concerns. *Inside Higher Education*. https://www.insidehighered.com/news/2018/10/29/cornell-ends-partnership-chinese-university-over-academic-freedom-concerns. Accessed December 17, 2018.

Open Access This chapter is licensed under the terms of the Creative Commons Attribution 4.0 International License (http://creativecommons.org/licenses/by/4.0/), which permits use, sharing, adaptation, distribution and reproduction in any medium or format, as long as you give appropriate credit to the original author(s) and the source, provide a link to the Creative Commons license and indicate if changes were made.

The images or other third party material in this chapter are included in the chapter's Creative Commons license, unless indicated otherwise in a credit line to the material. If material is not included in the chapter's Creative Commons license and your intended use is not permitted by statutory regulation or exceeds the permitted use, you will need to obtain permission directly from the copyright holder.

Long-Term Sustainability in Global Higher Education Partnerships

9

Michael Lanford

1 Introduction

The creation of a global partnership in education requires a considerable investment of time and resources, yet comparatively little attention is given to long-term sustainability. This is surprising because, even when partnerships make excellent "common sense," long-term sustainability can be negatively impacted by a number of factors, including inequitable levels of commitment, confusion about the partnership's objectives, and/or cultural misunderstandings [1–3]. Moreover, the process of leveraging the necessary expertise, resources, and human capital to forge a partnership is both time-consuming and costly [4, 5].

Drawing from extant literature on global research partnerships that detail the firsthand experiences of international branch campuses, transnational education agreements, research collaborations, and other multinational consortia arrangements, this chapter first identifies four specific threats to long-term sustainability. The first threat involves divergent motivations and goals for the partnership. The second threat is inadequate planning and funding volatility, especially in instances when a partnership is overly reliant on one source of funding and is susceptible to market forces. The third threat addresses the issue of leadership turnover and a lack of formal and informal leaders from within the partnership. The fourth threat concerns poor staff morale as the result of an over-reliance on part-time employment; limited opportunities for individual advancement; and/or differing expectations for shared governance, faculty duties, and academic freedom.

Afterward, the chapter proposes four conditions that can improve the prospects of long-term sustainability for colleges and universities interested in stable, mutually beneficial global partnerships. First, a careful, transparent analysis of both institutions' organizational cultures is essential so that an alignment in motivations and goals for both parties can be fostered. Second, multiple funding sources are vital, along with a strategic plan that outlines the projected duration of the partnership, prospects for deeper synergies, and entrepreneurial ventures. Third, shared leadership responsibilities among multiple individuals ensure consistent performance amidst turnover and change. Fourth, an environment that promotes dialog and opportunities for professional growth must be cultivated so that individuals feel like vested members of the partnership, concurrent with their membership in their respective disciplinary and professional communities.

As a final matter, the chapter considers two ethical issues pertinent to contemporary global partnerships. First, it argues that global partnerships should not simply exist in a vacuum, with benefits exclusively held by the members of the partnership. Instead, a global partnership should also forge a charter with society, fulfilling higher education's traditional outreach, instructional, and research missions so that the continued relevance of the partnership is apparent to internal and external stakeholders from a variety of backgrounds and experiences. Second, it maintains that activities related to innovation and entrepreneurship should be considered from the standpoint of the public good and conducted in a transparent manner, particularly if potential conflicts of interest might arise.

2 Threats to Long-Term Sustainability

In the early 1990s, researchers from the fields of business and marketing established an empirical basis for understanding why transnational collaborations either thrive or deteriorate over time. These researchers were motivated by a sense that globalization was rapidly transforming international trade, fostering a sense of interconnectedness between previously distant cultures, and encouraging competition for intellectual property and cheap labor between individual corporations

M. Lanford (✉)
University of North Georgia, Atlanta, USA
e-mail: Michael.Lanford@ung.edu

© The Author(s) 2020
A. AI-Youbi et al. (eds.), *Successful Global Collaborations in Higher Education Institutions*,
https://doi.org/10.1007/978-3-030-25525-1_9

and nation-states [6]. Therefore, they felt that new theoretical frameworks and data were necessary to depict changing business practices in a world of amplified entrepreneurial ventures and remarkable instability in labor markets.

Their conclusions were consistent in that healthy communication channels and trust were repeatedly found to be crucial for a productive and sustainable transnational relationship [7–10]. Collaborations that did not have these two essential ingredients were unlikely to survive threats to long-term sustainability that emerged at a surprisingly rapid pace, even during early interaction periods between stakeholders. Subsequent studies of global higher education partnerships have exhibited similar results, and four themes emerge from this evolving literature.

2.1 Divergent Motivations and Goals

The earliest factor highlighted by researchers concerned shared motivations and goals for the partnership [11]. As Heffernan and Poole discovered in their late-1990s studies of Australian universities' transnational partnerships, "quite simply, where there was a mismatch between the Australian university and the overseas education provider on the primary objectives and vision for the relationship, deterioration and potential termination in the relationship often occurred" [12]. In more recent years, the fate of several international branch campuses has suffered from similar mismatches between the aspirations of the home institution and the interests of the host country.

For example, the University of Nevada at Las Vegas (UNLV) offered undergraduate and graduate degrees in hospitality management and executive education for nearly ten years in the city-state of Singapore through an initially successful international branch campus venture. However, the branch campus was torn between the ambitions of UNLV (to establish a more comprehensive institution in an area perceived to have substantial economic promise and student talent) and the more circumspect plans of Singapore (to develop their own hospitality management program that could produce skilled labor for the city centerpiece Marina Bay Sands resort). Once the Singapore government no longer needed the expertise of UNLV's hospitality program, the international branch campus was forced to financially support itself through student tuition revenue. In subsequent years, the UNLV Singapore suffered from low visibility and paltry student enrollment, so it summarily closed [13].

2.2 Inadequate Planning and Funding Volatility

Institutions in Western nations where state funding for higher education has precipitously declined in recent years have been particularly keen to view global partnerships as an opportunity to generate much-needed income [14]. For example, Monash University in Australia unveiled international branch campuses in Malaysia and South Africa after its 1999 strategic development plan cited a need for greater institutional self-reliance in the face of decreased government funding [15]. Nevertheless, if a partnership is overly reliant on one source of funding, it could be upended by market forces, causing each of the vested parties to question their long-term commitment.

Wilkins and Huisman have further observed that some global partnerships, in the rush for alternative sources of revenue, have failed to adequately "understand the cultures and business practices in the regions they would like to operate" [16]. Drawing upon Simon Marginson's conceptualization of the Confucian higher education model in Southeast Asia [17], they explain how an incomplete understanding of cultural and political forces could result in frustration:

> In countries such as China, Korea, and Singapore, the Confucian model molds higher education systems. Although foreign higher education institutions might benefit from high levels of family commitment to investment in higher education, they need to be aware that the government retains tight control over policy, planning, and funding [16].

Additionally, regional differences in contract law, hiring practices, and financial accounting practices cause instability for global partnerships [18, 19]. As a result, global partnerships that are created without substantial planning and an interrogation of regional cultures and national regulatory frameworks are unlikely to succeed beyond the first few years.

2.3 Leadership Turnover and Instability

For global partnerships to remain viable, leaders must carefully balance competing demands from external and internal stakeholders who are likely to have different agendas and visions for the partnership. For instance, the host institution or country (an external stakeholder from the perspective of the partnering institutions) may want to control resources and influence hiring practices. Internal stakeholders, in turn, are likely to feel protective about outside influences over curricula, research programs, and branding efforts. For these reasons, leadership stability is extremely important in maintaining a consistent vision and trajectory for a global partnership [20].

Unfortunately, global partnerships have historically witnessed substantial turnover in administrative and executive positions. Further, the recruitment and retention of knowledgeable administrators essential to the partnership can prove to be difficult [21]. The pool of individuals who have the global perspective and administrative background to lead a transnational partnership is relatively small. And yet, even the individuals who have the necessary experience to lead a global partnership may be loath to rebuild professional contacts in a new environment while uprooting their domestic partners and children from their professional careers and extended families.

As a final note, organizations can have a variety of expectations concerning leadership norms. Educational institutions, however, are different from many organizations in that a certain degree of freedom and collegiality is frequently expected by administrators and executives. Some may even be attracted to a global partnership specifically because they think greater workplace freedom may result from a group that is loosely coupled to multiple organizations, rather than intricately tied to a single institution [22].

Nonetheless, Anatoly Oleksiyenko has wisely cautioned that "corporate abuse emerges and is sustained primarily in zones of alienation—places with poorly designed academic organization, which fail to safeguard academic freedom, respect, and healthy collegial relations" [23]. The specific location where a global partnership largely conducts its work may have a culture that is more entrenched in hierarchical decision-making, and it could find its momentum stymied by frustrated employees who are used to greater independence in their previous jobs.

2.4 Poor Faculty and Staff Morale

Similar to the topic of leadership, Phillip Altbach has argued that recruiting and keeping faculty talent in global partnerships is the "greatest problem of sustainability":

> [Faculty are] reluctant to leave their work, especially in the sciences. Junior faculty worry that overseas teaching will not serve their chances for promotion. Concerns about the education of children, employment of spouses, and other family issues also intervene. Even in cases where additional remuneration and other benefits are offered, it is frequently difficult to lure professors overseas. The problem is exacerbated over time. The relatively small number of home-campus faculty willing to relocate is restricted and quickly exhausted [24].

It is also known that the expectations of shared governance [25], faculty duties and participation [26], and academic freedom [27] may differ significantly among cross-border partners. This leads to cognitive dissonance among faculty who assume that the governance, service expectations, and freedom they experienced in their past institutional environments will continue unabated in a different cultural realm.

Since full-time faculty are often difficult to recruit for a global partnership, part-time faculty are frequently hired to fill teaching (and occasionally research) positions. However, an over-reliance on part-time faculty could limit teaching effectiveness, research productivity, and opportunities for individual advancement [28]. Part-time employees are also less likely to commit to a single institution. Compounding the problem is the fact that there is generally an unwillingness for global partnerships to be forthright about the challenges faculty will face in a foreign environment [29].

3 Improving the Prospects for Long-Term Sustainability

Given the confluence of these challenges, one might reasonably wonder if a global partnership is all but doomed beyond the first couple of years. This chapter, though, takes a different position. It contends that the threats to long-term sustainability outlined in the previous section can be ameliorated, but only if careful steps are taken to plan the future of the partnership, determine the organizational culture, distribute leadership responsibilities, and promote open dialog and professional growth.

3.1 Alignment in Motivations and Goals for Both Parties

He and Wilkins have suggested that to achieve legitimacy, international branch campuses have been compelled to "follow the local regulations of either the host country government or the quality assurance bodies," creating a situation where "the curriculum of the international branch campus must conform to the local standards" [30]. Thus, any type of global partnership is placed in a bind, whereby different legitimacy building strategies must be strategically considered. Some may argue that the partnership should simply conform to local practices, as He and Wilkins have documented. Others may assert that the partnership can establish independence if nearby institutional forces are weak and there is a low dependence on local resources.

This chapter instead contends that both parties need to have a similar investment in the motivations and goals of a partnership. For this to occur, at least three steps should be undertaken. First, a careful, open analysis should be conducted of both institutions' organizational cultures. Location can certainly influence this discussion; as described by Healey, "transnational education partnerships often operate in the rapidly growing economies of the Middle-East and Asia, where the linguistic, cultural, political, and legislative environments are very foreign to those of the exporting universities" [31].

Second, an equitable distribution of staff and coherent hiring practices should be cultivated. When too many employees come from one institution, the strengths of the partnership (e.g., diversity of ideas, a multicultural perspective) are diluted. Also, there is a risk that the organizational culture and mission statement will be undermined by the belief systems and past experiences of the majority group.

Third, the joint development of a mission statement should guide partnership activities. For all educational institutions, mission statements are of exceptional significance, as they can regulate the allocation of resources, accentuate certain organizational activities, and provide a sense of clarity during turbulent times. Without a clear mission, the partnership may lack coherence, and stakeholders will question its relevance.

3.2 Careful Planning and Multiple Funding Sources

Along with the development of a mission statement, a strategic plan should outline the projected duration of the partnership. In a study of 60 global higher education partnerships, Mwangi found "ninety percent of partnership stakeholders cited that a critical aspect of a successful partnership was the deliberate time and attention given to planning before implementation as it allowed for the development of effective and realistic goals for the project" [32]. Thus, the strategic plan should be formulated well before any official partnership activities take place and substantial financial resources are apportioned. By the same token, all institutions should have relatively equitable investments—of both money and resources—in the success of the partnership. As the strategic plan is developed, prospects for deeper synergies, entrepreneurial ventures, and/or other partners should be identified.

3.3 Shared Leadership Responsibilities

If global partnerships are destined to have significant leadership turnover, then it may appear virtually impossible to cultivate a consistent institutional identity and nurture values endemic to the organization. One solution, however, is to adopt distributed leadership theories that encourage individuals throughout the organization to become experts at specific areas essential for daily operations while concurrently developing leadership skills [33]. While no one leadership style is ideal for every organizational culture, the sharing of leadership responsibilities is important for reliable performance amidst turnover and change. This is especially true for relatively small organizations, like global partnerships, that have difficulty in cultivating "buy-in" among employees.

The communication style of leaders should also be consistent and effective in the local context. As Borgos [29] has noted, "the success of an organization in part will depend on its ability to make connections within the host country and to manage its dependency on the foreign external environment in which it operates". Without leadership who can forcefully articulate the goals and values of the partnership, the host culture might face difficulties in delivering appropriate support.

As a final point, not all leaders of an institution hold titles that signify their leadership credentials. Every institution has discernible "informal" leaders who may not hold an explicit leadership role but are widely recognized by their peers as important representatives of employee sentiments and as conduits for information about institutional decisions. Any partnership that hopes to maintain a sense of continuity from one year to the next cannot ignore the influence and prominence of these "informal" leaders. Instead, an institution needs to identify both the "formal" and "informal" leaders within the organization so that strategic decisions are deliberated and implemented in a manner that makes people feel that their sentiments—and their hard work—are valued [34].

3.4 Open Dialog and Professional Growth

Finally, a global partnership should be an environment that promotes open dialog and encourages opportunities for individual professional growth. The expectations of governance, faculty activities, and free speech (for all members, including faculty, staff, and students) should be clear, especially if they differ from the expectations of the partners' campuses. In addition, it is essential to remember that researchers are members of the partnership and also members of their scholarly communities; they need to have opportunities for personal and professional growth in both spheres. For some individuals interested in developing their teaching expertise, this might mean participation and financial support for pedagogical seminars and instructional colloquia in different countries. For faculty who wish to maintain their research profile, grant funding support and institutional sponsorship of faculty and student research collaborations might be necessary.

Similarly, administrative and staff professionals will likely maintain a duality in which they devote substantial energy to the preservation of distant professional relationships while they further the immediate goals of the partnership. Such a division of roles should not be seen as a distraction; rather, it should be encouraged as a way to both develop the skills of partnership members and spread the activities of the partnership to new audiences [35].

4 Establishing Legitimacy by Embracing Community

Over the past 20 years, global higher education partnerships have expanded due to several motivating factors grounded in rational planning and global competition. From the perspective of the "host" country, a global partnership can be one vital component of a broader strategy to expand capacity in the higher education sector, develop a twenty-first-century workforce, encourage collaborative research, or enhance institutional prestige. From the perspective of the "exporting" institution, a global partnership can propel institutional branding efforts, forge international ties, lead to the recruitment of talented students and faculty, or simply be financially advantageous.

4.1 Legitimacy Concerns

Despite these potential benefits, global partnerships continue to suffer from internal and external legitimacy concerns. The faculty and staff of exporting institutions regularly question the purposes and value systems of global partnerships and, at times, actively campaign against their development. Those who work in a global partnership may not only feel distant from the activities and reward structures on their home campuses but also acutely aware of the opposition to their work. The benefits to the majority of people in the host country are also too frequently unclear, as global partnerships may appear to have little engagement with their surrounding communities [36].

Therefore, it is useful to ask if the discussion around global partnerships in higher education has been, to date, far too circumscribed by neoliberal philosophies that extol economic gain and competitive advantage. Partnerships are almost always formed between inherently unequal parties. One only needs to observe the number of global partnerships between institutions from wealthy nations and institutions from low-income countries, along with the resultant uneven levels of participation and individual agency [37]. The imbalances in North–South research collaborations that grant Northern researchers the ability to establish research priorities, dictate the theories to be deployed, and decide the methods to be utilized have also been well-documented [38].

Additionally, as Phillip Altbach and Jane Knight have cautioned, "globalization tends to concentrate wealth, knowledge, and power in those already possessing these elements" [39]. Authors have extended this analysis to observe that global partnerships and international branch campuses reify elite global university networks while having a limited (perhaps even negative) impact on educational equity and basic human rights, such as free speech and the protection of minoritized people [40–42].

Conversely, an increasing number of research studies have demonstrated that transnational higher education has a minimal, if not completely ineffectual, impact on local educational entities due to a lack of inter-institutional communication and knowledge exchange [43]. Global higher education partnerships have also tended to operate outside of traditional regulatory environments in that they operate as private entities (even when they receive public funding), and they have nebulous accountability to both their home institutions and their respective governments [44]. These findings are especially disquieting for those countries who hope global partnerships will stimulate education hubs, a region distinguished by an expansion of cross-border talent, knowledge production, and innovative ideas that can have immediate, tangible benefits for the local economy and society as a whole [45].

4.2 Conceptualizing a Charter with Society

Hence, this chapter takes a different conceptual perspective by asking a final question: What would it look like if global partnerships in higher education developed a charter with their respective societies?

As Kezar has compellingly argued, contemporary higher education is torn between key aspects of neoliberalism, such as private enterprise and economic enterprise, and traditional notions of the public good, where colleges and universities support local and regional communities through contributions to government, health care, primary education, and other social institutions [46]. However, it is important to emphasize that neoliberal values and the public good need not be in perpetual conflict. In fact, global higher education partnerships may need to refocus some of their neoliberal activities in service of the public good in order to establish greater legitimacy and assuage critics who feel such partnerships are only advancing the aspirations of elite actors and institutions.

One way to accomplish such a task is to perform educational outreach activities in local communities. Elsewhere, I have written about how international branch campuses can be too often viewed as cloistered communities that preserve valuable educational resources for a privileged few [47]. Global higher education partnerships could instead embrace, particularly in their mission statements, the responsibility to train globally minded citizens. Furthermore, outreach efforts could be maintained with local community organizations to provide support for marginalized groups that might otherwise be overlooked or exploited.

Second, the fruits of artistic endeavor and scientific development should be available to individuals in the community, as well as members of the partnership and sponsoring institutions. A global partnership should not have an exclusive focus on enriching the coffers of the institutional stakeholders. A long-term goal of greater access could be simultaneously developed so that the partnership is truly a hub for diverse backgrounds and perspectives—not just a multicultural collection of elite actors.

Third, activities related to innovation and entrepreneurship should be conducted in a transparent manner, particularly if they invite potential conflicts of interest. The temptation to monetize every innovation is understandable, given the competitive pressures of globalization, university rankings, and academic branding efforts. A compact with society, though, would weigh short-term benefits related to resources and prestige with the long-term sustainability of a partnership that is perceived as being vital for societal progress [48]. If an innovation or important medical discovery becomes too expensive for most people in the surrounding community to use, then the partnership has behaved no differently than a multinational corporation beholden to shareholders.

5 Conclusion

A global partnership in higher education can strengthen existing academic networks and business relationships [49], promote greater intercultural awareness [50], and open new opportunities for innovative research [51]. Despite their continued expansion, however, such partnerships are plagued by poor planning, sustainability problems, and legitimacy concerns. Many partnerships seem to be created only with a short-term perspective that is set up to take advantage of temporary financial windfalls and/or human capital that is susceptible to exploitation. Once the slightest difficulty threatens the partnership's survival, it may be ill-equipped to articulate a coherent mission, transition to alternative funding sources, rely on a combination of "formal" and "informal" leaders, or foster open dialog, each of which have been proven to sustain organizations for the long term.

Moreover, power dynamics between different transnational educational stakeholders remains a topic worthy of continued investigation. As this chapter has demonstrated, a global higher education partnership must carefully negotiate cultural expectations and norms, consider the perspectives of different partners, and ensure that communication channels are maintained, particularly for those who might reside in marginalized positions within the organization. What we have learned over the past two decades of global higher education partnerships is that competition too often obscures original intent—and the intent is to sustain a mutually beneficial alliance that will not only advance the dreams and ambitions of individuals within the organization, but ultimately benefit society as well.

References

1. Healey, N. (2018). The optimal global integration-local responsiveness tradeoff for an international branch campus. *Research in Higher Education, 59*(5), 623–649.
2. Healey, N. (2015). Towards a risk-based typology for transnational education. *Higher Education, 69*(1), 1–18.
3. Tierney, W. G., & Lanford, M. (2015). An investigation of the impact of international branch campuses on organizational culture. *Higher Education, 70*(2), 283–298.
4. Knight, J. (2011). Education hubs: A fad, a brand, an innovation? *Journal of Studies in International Education, 15*(2), 221–240.
5. Oleksiyenko, A., & Sá, C. (2010). Resource asymmetries and cumulative advantages: Canadian and U.S. research universities and the field of global health. *Higher Education, 59*(3), 367–385.
6. Held, D., McGrew, A., Goldblatt, D., & Perraton, J. (1999). *Global transformations: Politics, economics, and culture*. Stanford, CA: Stanford University Press.
7. Anderson, J. C., & Narus, J. A. (1990). A model of distributor firm and manufacturer firm working partnerships. *Journal of Marketing, 54*(1), 42–58.
8. Czepiel, J. (1990). Service encounters and service relationships: Implications for research. *Journal of Business Research, 20,* 13–21.
9. Morgan, R. M., & Hunt, S. D. (1994). The commitment-trust theory of relationship marketing. *Journal of Marketing, 58*(3), 20–38.
10. Webster, F. E. (1992). The changing role of marketing in the corporation. *Journal of Marketing, 56*(4), 1–17.
11. Heffernan, T., & Poole, D. (2005). In search of "the vibe": Creating effective international education partnerships. *Higher Education, 50*(2), 223–245.
12. Heffernan, T., & Poole, D. (2004). "Catch me I'm falling": Key factors in the deterioration of offshore education partnerships. *Journal of Higher Education Policy and Management, 26*(1), 75–90.
13. Weinman, J. (2019). *The case of UNLV Singapore: Lessons learned from an international branch campus closure*. Paper presented at the Comparative and International Education Society Annual Conference, San Francisco, USA.
14. Welch, A. (2011). *Higher education in Southeast Asia: Blurring borders, changing balance*. Abingdon: Routledge.
15. McBurnie, G., & Pollock, A. (2000). Opportunity and risk in transnational education—Issues in planning for international campus development: An Australian perspective. *Higher Education in Europe, 25*(3), 333–343.
16. Wilkins, S., & Huisman, J. (2012). The international branch campus as transnational strategy in higher education. *Higher Education, 64*(5), 627–645.
17. Marginson, S. (2011). Higher education in East Asia and Singapore: Rise of the Confucian model. *Higher Education, 61* (5), 587–611.
18. Harding, L. M., & Lammey, R. W. (2011). Operational considerations for opening a branch campus abroad. *New Directions for Higher Education, 155,* 65–78.

19. Verbik, L. (2007). The international branch campus: Models and trends. *International Higher Education, 46,* 14–15.
20. Lane, J. (2011). Global expansion of international branch campuses: Managerial and leadership challenges. *New Directions for Higher Education, 155,* 5–7.
21. Shams, F., & Huisman, J. (2014). The role of institutional dual embeddedness in the strategic local adaptation of international branch campuses: Evidence from Malaysia and Singapore. *Studies in Higher Education, 41*(6), 955–970.
22. Weick, K. E. (1976). Educational organizations as loosely coupled systems. *Administrative Science Quarterly, 21*(1), 1–19.
23. Oleksiyenko, A. (2018). Zones of alienation in global higher education: Corporate abuse and leadership failures. *Tertiary Education and Management, 24*(3), 193–205.
24. Altbach, P. (2010). Why branch campuses may be unsustainable. *International Higher Education, 58,* 2–3.
25. Healey, N. (2008). Is higher education in really "internationalizing?". *Higher Education, 55*(3), 333–355.
26. McBurnie, G., & Ziguras, C. (2007). *Transnational education: Issues and trends in off-shore higher education.* London: Routledge.
27. Tierney, W. G., & Lanford, M. (2014). The question of academic freedom: Universal right or relative term? *Frontiers of Education in China, 9*(1), 4–23.
28. Kinser, K., et al. (2010). *The global growth of higher education.* San Francisco: Wiley.
29. Borgos, J. (2016). Addressing sustainable international branch campus development through an organizational structure lens: A comparative analysis of China, Qatar, and the United Arab Emirates. *Chinese Education and Society, 49*(4–5), 271–287.
30. He, L., & Wilkins, S. (2017). Achieving legitimacy in cross-border higher education: Institutional influences on Chinese international branch campuses in South East Asia. *Journal of Studies in International Education, 22*(3), 179–197.
31. Healey, N. (2018). The challenges of managing transnational education partnerships: The views of "home-based" managers vs. "in-country" managers. *International Journal of Educational Management, 32*(2), 241–256.
32. Mwangi, C. A. G. (2017). Partner positioning: Examining international higher education partnerships through a mutuality lens. *Review of Higher Education, 41*(1), 33–60.
33. Spillane, J. P. (2005). Distributed leadership. *Educational Forum, 69*(2), 143–150.
34. Tierney, W. G., & Lanford, M. (2018). Institutional culture in higher education. In J. C. Shin & P. N. Teixeira (Eds.), *Encyclopedia of international higher education systems and institutions* (pp. 1–7). Dordrecht: Springer.
35. Cai, L., & Hall, C. (2016). Motivations, expectations, and experiences of expatriate academic staff on an international branch campus in China. *Journal of Studies in International Education, 20*(3), 207–222.
36. Siltaoja, M., Juusola, K., & Kivijärvi, M. (2018). "World-class" fantasies: A neocolonial analysis of international branch campuses. *Organization,* 1–23 (advance online publication).
37. Leng, P. (2016). Mutuality in Cambodian international university partnerships: Looking beyond the global discourse. *Higher Education, 72*(3), 261–275.
38. Koehn, P. H. (2013). Developments in transnational research linkages: Evidence from U.S. higher education activity. *New Approaches in Educational Research, 3*(2), 52–58.
39. Altbach, P., & Knight, J. (2007). The internationalization of higher education: Motivations and realities. *Journal of Studies in International Education, 11*(3–4), 290–305.
40. Altbach, P., & Hazelkorn, E. (2017). Pursuing rankings in the age of massification: For most—forget about it. *International Higher Education, 89,* 8–10.
41. Pusser, B., & Marginson, S. (2013). University rankings in critical perspective. *Journal of Higher Education, 84*(4), 544–568.
42. Tierney, W. G., & Lanford, M. (2017). Between massification and globalization: Is there a role for global university rankings? In E. Hazelkorn (Ed.), *Global rankings and the geopolitics of higher education* (pp. 295–308). Oxford: Routledge.
43. Ding, X. (2018). Marginal revolution: The impact of transnational education on higher education in host countries: A case study of China. *Higher Education Policy,* 1–22. https://doi.org/10.1057/s41307-018-0089-5.
44. Lane, J., & Kinser, K. (2008). The private nature of cross-border higher education. *International Higher Education, 53,* 11.
45. Knight, J. (2018). International education hubs. In P. Meusburger, M. Heffernan, & L. Suarsana (Eds.), *Geographies of the university* (pp. 637–655). Cham: Springer.
46. Kezar, A. (2004). Obtaining integrity? Reviewing and examining the charter between higher education and society. *Review of Higher Education, 27*(4), 429–459.
47. Lanford, M., & Tierney, W. G. (2016). The international branch campus: Cloistered community or agent of social change? In D. Neubauer, J. Hawkins, M. Lee, & C. Collins (Eds.), *The Palgrave handbook of Asia Pacific higher education* (pp. 157–172). New York: Palgrave Macmillan.
48. Tierney, W. G., & Lanford, M. (2016). Conceptualizing innovation in higher education. In M. B. Paulsen (Ed.), *Higher education: Handbook of theory and research* (Vol. 31, pp. 1–40). Dordrecht: Springer.
49. Kim, J., & Celis, S. (2016). Global partnership as a strategy for internationalisation: MBAs in Latin America and Asia and Oceania. *Higher Education Policy, 29*(3), 355–378.
50. DeLong, M., et al. (2011). Cultural exchange: Evaluating an alternative model in higher education. *Journal of Studies in International Education, 15*(1), 41–56.
51. Tierney, W. G., & Lanford, M. (2016). *Cultivating strategic innovation in higher education.* New York: TIAA-CREF Institute.

Open Access This chapter is licensed under the terms of the Creative Commons Attribution 4.0 International License (http://creativecommons.org/licenses/by/4.0/), which permits use, sharing, adaptation, distribution and reproduction in any medium or format, as long as you give appropriate credit to the original author(s) and the source, provide a link to the Creative Commons license and indicate if changes were made.

The images or other third party material in this chapter are included in the chapter's Creative Commons license, unless indicated otherwise in a credit line to the material. If material is not included in the chapter's Creative Commons license and your intended use is not permitted by statutory regulation or exceeds the permitted use, you will need to obtain permission directly from the copyright holder.